Working with Children
in
Grief and Loss

Working with Children in Grief and Loss

edited by

Bruce Lindsay

BA (Hons), RSCN, RGN, Cert Ed
Lecturer in Child Care
School of Nursing and Midwifery
University of East Anglia, Norwich

John Elsegood

B Ed(Hons), RMN, RGN
Senior Lecturer
School of Nursing and Midwifery
University of East Anglia, Norwich

Baillière Tindall
LONDON PHILADELPHIA TORONTO TOKYO SYDNEY

Baillière Tindall   24–28 Oval Road
London NW1 7DX

The Curtis Center
Independence Square West
Philadelphia, PA 19106-3399, USA

Harcourt Brace & Company
55 Horner Avenue
Toronto, Ontario, M8Z 4X6, Canada

Harcourt Brace & Company, Australia
30–52 Smidmore Street
Marrickville
NSW 2204, Australia

Harcourt Brace & Company, Japan
Ichibancho Central Building
22–1 Ichibancho
Chiyoda-ku, Tokyo 102, Japan

A catalogue record for this book is available from the British Library

ISBN 0-7020-1960-7

Typeset by WestKey Ltd, Falmouth, Cornwall
Printed and bound in Great Britain by Hartnolls Ltd, Bodmin, Cornwall

Contents

Contributors

Lilian Beattie, MB, BS, MFCH, DHP
Retired Senior Clinical Medical Officer (Child Health)
Director and Consultant for Adlerian Workshops and Publications
Counsellor and Psychotherapist in Private Practice
Coniston House
36 Dobbins Lane
Wendover
Bucks HP22 6DH

Marian Brandon, MA, CQSW
University Lecturer
School of Health and Social Work
University of East Anglia
Norwich NR4 7TJ

Elizabeth Capewell, MA (Cantab), PGCE, Dip Hum Psych, Cert
Counselling
Director, Centre for Crisis Management and Education
Roselyn House
93 Old Newtown Road
Newbury, Berkshire RG14 7DE

Penny Cook, RSCN, Cert Counselling and Group Work
Family Liaison Sister
Children's Services
Box 181, Addenbrookes Hospital
Hills Road, Cambridge CB2 2QQ

John Elsegood, B Ed(Hons), RMN, RGN
Senior Lecturer
School of Nursing and Midwifery
University of East Anglia
Norwich
NR4 7TJ

Bridget Hallam BSc, RGN, RHV
5 Chapel Lane
Leasingham
Sleaford
Lincolnshire NG34 8LB

Yvonne Gabell, MA(Oxon), Cert Ed
Counsellor in Private Practice
51 Beeston Common
Sheringham
Norfolk NR26 8EU

Bruce Lindsay BA (Hons), RSCN, RGN, Cert Ed
School of Nursing and Midwifery
University of East Anglia
Norwich
NR4 7TJ

Betty Rathbone, MA, M Phil, Dip Psych
Retired Chartered Clinical Psychologist
50 Elm Grove lane
Norwich NR3 3LF

Gillian Schofield, MA, MSW, CQSW
University Lecturer
School of Health and Social Work
University of East Anglia
Norwich NR4 7TJ

Penny Vine, SRN, School Nursing Certificate
School Nurse,
Boston Health Clinic,
Lincoln Lane,
Boston, Lincolnshire PE21 8RU

Preface

This is a book for child care professionals who may be faced every day with children who are suffering loss. It is a book which aims to enable these professionals to deal more effectively with the grief which these children suffer. It is not intended to make every child care professional an expert in dealing with children's grief, but to increase their awareness of grief, their ability to deal with this grief and their understanding of when expert help is needed and how to obtain this help.

Much of the current literature on children's loss focusses on situations of bereavement or terminal illness. This is of course a vital area of child care and is considered by many of the contributors to this volume. However, in modern Western societies it is relatively rare for a child to be dealing with loss through death. Grief occasioned by other types of loss is far commoner and for an individual child may be equally devastating. Loss is inherent in a wide range of social, educational, domestic, legislative and medical situations to which children are exposed. Acute and chronic illness, disability, hospitalisation, divorce, starting a new school, moving to a new neighbourhood, homelessness and poverty, school examination results and career interviews, adoption, going into foster care, changing foster parents, and separation from a parent who works abroad or is in prison, or from a sibling who moves away from home are just a few examples.

These losses often appear to remain unidentified by professionals and even when they are recognised our responses often fall short of what the grieving child needs. Correct support at an early stage of grieving may be of vital importance for the child, preventing abnormal grieving and avoiding the need for specialist intervention. We hope that the information in this book will help readers to develop their skills and understanding.

The book opens with two chapters focussing on development. The first discusses the development of society's (and in particular health professionals') changing responses to children's grief. The second looks at development in relation to loss and grief. The remaining chapters are practically-orientated, spanning a range of topics such as planning for situations of loss, identifying and responding to grief, and breaking bad news. The book ends with a brief list of sources of further information: a list of organisations rather than a comprehensive list of books, videos and other resources, for this is a rapidly developing field which quickly renders lists of such resources incomplete and out of date. Throughout the book the terms "child" and "children" are used in their broadest sense to include adolescents as well as younger children: where necessary, reference is made to specific age groups.

The chapters of this book are written mainly with health professionals in mind, but focus on situations which are often experienced by other child care professionals in their own areas of practice, such as education or social work. These professionals too should find material which is of interest and of use. The contributors to "Working with children in grief and loss" come from a variety of backgrounds and the material is enriched and its application broadened by the different perspectives they bring.

The book is designed as a "Reader" rather than as a comprehensive text and the chapters can be read singly, in any order or in any combination according to the needs or interests of the individual reader. However, the chapters are sequenced in such a way as to provide coherence and a logical development for the reader who wishes to progress through the chapters in the order in which they are presented.

In particular, this book focusses on meeting the needs of the child. It is a "child-centered" rather than "family-centered" text: a perspective which may not find favour with many child care professionals for who the terms child and family are almost synonymous.

"Working with children in grief and loss" is the result of much effort by many people. Our thanks go to our colleagues and friends who have contributed comments and suggestions, to Sarah James and Robert Langham, our editors, and the staff at Baillière Tindall, and, of course, to our contributors. Most of all our thanks go to our families and in particular to Julie, Sam, Alex, Vivienne, Christopher, Jonathan and Eileen for the support, understanding and insights they have given during the book's creation.

Bruce Lindsay
John Elsegood
Norwich, November 1995

1
An Historical Perspective

Bruce Lindsay

This chapter looks at some of the changing perspectives on children's grief, within the context of changing ideas about childhood and about the child's place in society. This is a complex subject, involving factors such as the nature of childhood, the changing experiences of children's lives, developments in health care and alterations to family life and child-rearing. The discussion here will focus in particular on health professionals' responses to children's grief, in order to establish an historical base for later discussions.

A book which focuses on health professionals' work with grieving children may be said to make certain assumptions. It assumes that children's grief needs dealing with in different ways from adults' grief (and, consequently, that children's grief differs from adults' grief). It assumes that health professionals are appropriate people to deal with children's grief. It assumes that dealing with children's grief is an appropriate role for health professionals. And it assumes that children are neither able or obliged to deal with their own grief unaided. This is an accepted contemporary view, fitting with relative ease into notions of specialist child health care professionals and family-centred care.

Such a view is not the 'right view'. It is simply the current perspective on this particular aspect of children's lives, stemming from our current perspective on children and childhood in general. Childhood is a difficult concept to define: what was 'childhood' to people in the nineteenth century may not be recognisable to people of the late twentieth century. As Phillips (1994, p. 62) notes, 'Childhood is a relatively modern invention', one which is not static, but varies through time according to changing social conditions. If one accepts this idea of childhood as socially constructed then the problem of definition becomes more than a theoretical argument, it becomes fundamental to any understanding of historical changes in a society's response to and treatment of its children.

This chapter concentrates in particular on the century from 1850–1950. This period begins with the establishment of Britain's first specialist children's hospitals, which started with the Hospital for Sick Children, Great Ormond Street (GOS), in 1852. It ends with the establishment of the National Health Service and the publication of early research into maternal deprivation and separation by authorities such as John Bowlby (1969) and James Robertson (Robertson and Robertson, 1989), whose work was eventually to influence much of our current perspective on the health care of children.

Changing Childhood

Whatever a particular society understands as the 'nature of childhood' will affect its responses to the experiences of children. Where this understanding changes through time then so, too, will those responses. Until relatively recently the child in Western society was indistinguishable from the adult in many aspects of everyday life (Phillips, 1994). Once the period of weaning had ended and the child was able to perform basic tasks such as eating and dressing independently, the child's world became that of the adult. While allowances had to be made for a child's relative lack of physical strength, this did not excuse them from the work, religious or recreational activities which were part of life regardless of age.

By the eighteenth century the differentiation of children from adults was well under way. Aries suggests that this was due at least in part to a developing interest in education coupled with a change in the role of the family from one as 'an institution for the transmission of a name and an estate' to one with 'a moral and spiritual function, it moulded bodies and souls' (Aries, 1973). As a result of this combination, according to Aries,

> Henceforth it was recognised that the child was not ready for life, and that he had to be subjected to a special treatment, a sort of quarantine, before he was allowed to join the adults . . . Family and school together removed the child from adult society. (Aries, 1973, pp. 396–397).

Aries's viewpoint focuses on middle class and aristocratic families rather than on the poorer majority, who would have had little estate to transmit. However, the ideals of the middle and upper classes did filter through society (Hendrick, 1990) and ultimately this vision of children as worthy of 'special treatment' predominated. In Britain, the move to separate children from adults within the labour market and to bring them instead within the bounds of a national system of education grew during the mid-nineteenth century as the social environment developed to change some of the most crucial aspects of children's experience.

One explanation of the changing social construction of childhood in Britain is that of Hendrick (1990). Hendrick's discussion focuses on four interrelated themes and applies to the period from the end of the eighteenth century to the late twentieth century. The universalisation of the developing notion of childhood was achieved by 1918, suggests Hendrick. Through a combination of social, economic and political factors, children of all classes and from all corners of Britain were subject to the same constraints on their activities:

> In 1800 the meaning of childhood was ambiguous and not universally in demand. By 1914 the uncertainty had been resolved and the identity determined, at least to the satisfaction of the middle class and the respectable working class. . . . childhood was *legally, legislatively, socially, medically, psychologically, educationally and politically institutionalised* (1990, p. 36, my emphasis).

While Hendrick views the development of concepts of childhood as ongoing, other authorities have focused on what they have seen as crucial periods in this development. Jean S. Heywood (in the 1969 Convocation Lecture for the National Children's Home) identified the 1860s as a crucial decade of change regarding society's responses to children. This decade was, for her, 'the beginning of social justice for children, stimulated by the high mortality and waste of child life . . . and the obvious exploitation and misery of the poor' (Heywood, 1969, p. 56). It was a 'watershed' between the early Victorian culture of 'moral rigidity for the young' with its acceptance of strict and often violent discipline and the more liberal approaches of the 1870s and beyond when children became recognised as individuals with their own rights.

Lionel Rose, while also recognising the changes to society's ideas about childhood which stemmed from this period, is less optimistic about the immediacy of their resulting improvements. He identifies many examples of continued cruelty, exploitation and neglect until well into the twentieth century (Rose, 1991).

These ideas offer us explanations for the change in the way society viewed children and enable us to understand how our current beliefs about children have been developed. The precise pathway down which we have developed our current beliefs is open to argument. But in health care at least, this development offers a fascinating insight into our changing perspectives on children's grief.

The Changing Place of Children in Society

The century from 1850 saw many major changes to the place of children in British society. These changes helped to produce a population of children whose daily lives by the mid-twentieth century were far removed from those of 100 years previously. By 1888, 38 British children's hospitals had been established (White Franklin, 1964). The development of specialist fields of nursing and medicine alongside this growth in specialist hospitals meant for the first time that children were seen as having a discrete set of health care needs which could be met, at least in part, by the new and increasingly hospital-centred medical establishment. Community-centred specialists also came to the fore from the late nineteenth century onwards, with the development of Health Visiting, School Nursing and the Schools Medical Service, focusing on prevention and monitoring roles. Child welfare services also developed in the educational and social services, in both statutory and voluntary sectors.

The differentiation of children from adults, already largely completed by 1850 in terms of age-boundaries, led on to the differentiation of children's emotional responses from those of adults. The care of children in terms of their education, health and social well-being, became professionalised. Many aspects of this care, beyond the care of physically sick children, became medicalised and were taken into the domain of the new child health professions of paediatrics, child psychiatry and others.

A grieving child in 1850 is likely to have been cared for by the family, with support from neighbours and perhaps the Church. The care such a child would have received, and in many cases there may have been little if any care offered, may well have differed from that offered to adults only in the cases of very young children. The grieving child of the 1950s would have found a vast array of education, welfare and medical professionals ready to assess, test, diagnose and treat, with the idea that the problems and the solutions would be different from those of an adult. The child in the 1990s who suffers loss will find that professionalisation of care has continued, with the professionals becoming even more specialised. The intervention of specialist counsellors following traumatic events or major losses is now an accepted part of care for grieving children, perhaps reflecting a view of children's grief as no longer an appropriate problem for 'everyday' child care professionals to deal with.

The Child in the Family

For much of this period the family was viewed as the ideal unit for child-rearing, particularly by the middle class where the 'convention of the time took for granted that the proper context of childhood was the family' (Davin, 1978). What constituted 'the family' was not necessarily a constant: wealthy families would have expected a large part of the burden of child rearing to be undertaken by paid servants. Poorer families may have shared child care between siblings or extended family members, or with neighbouring families. When children became ill the responsibility for their care would have remained in the majority of cases with the people who cared for them when they were well.

Care which did involve health professionals was still predominantly carried out at home, on the instructions of a visiting physician or on the advice of a doctor in a dispensary or outpatients department, perhaps by a nurse if the family could afford one. Hospitalisation was far less common and was normally reserved for children when home care was no longer possible.

A child's experience of loss would have come in many of the same ways as it does today. The death of a pet, the loss of friends on moving home, or separation from parents due to work commitments (or due to a move to boarding school for children from wealthier families) all happened to children then as now. For a far higher proportion of children, particularly in the nineteenth century, loss would also come with the death of family members.

Surviving Infancy

One of the most marked, and remarkable, changes in British society over the century from 1850 was the huge fall in the child mortality rate (see Table 1.1). This fall can be clearly identified from the statistical evidence and, when considered in the population as a whole, presents a picture of a universally influential effect on demography, on average life expectancy and on the social expectations of individuals throughout the country.

The fall in child mortality was not a simple, gradual and egalitarian change, however. The rate of fall fluctuated greatly, was markedly different across the classes and showed great variation across urban and rural centres, across geographical boundaries and across different age bands (infant mortality rates in particular show patterns of change unlike those for children in other age groups). However, it served, along with other social factors, to reduce family size and to reduce the likelihood that children would have to deal from an early age with the deaths of brothers, sisters and friends. Parents too gradually came to the situation where the production of fewer children and the survival of a greater proportion of them helped to make children more precious. This also may have helped to change society's view of children, to make childhood a longer, more dependent period of life, and to make a child's grief a more specialist problem.

Table 1.1 England and Wales: death-rates 1851–1945 (per 1000 living in each age group, infant mortality per 1000 live births)

	Infant mortality*	Age group (years)		
		1–5	5–10	10–15
1851–1860	154	36.1(?)	8.5	5.0
1871–1880	149	31.2	6.5	3.7
1891–1900	153	24.3	4.3	2.5
1911–1915	110	16.2	3.4	2.1
1921–1925	76	10.3	2.5	1.7
1931–1935	62	6.6	2.2	1.4
1940	57	4.8	2.0	1.4
1941	60	5.3	2.1	1.4
1942	51	3.4	1.5	1.0
1943	49	3.3	1.4	1.0
1944	45	2.8	1.4	1.1
1945	46	2.6	1.2	0.9

Adapted from Ministry of Education (1947, p. 53).
*Based on related live births from 1931.

Children, Separation and Loss:
The Health Professionals' Perspective

The emotional needs of sick children are considered of paramount importance by late twentieth century health professionals. The emotional problems which may arise from a period of separation are recognised and care is planned to minimise them whenever possible. But were these problems of any less importance to the professionals of earlier years? The opinions of health professionals regarding the grief caused by separation are difficult to discover, particularly in the nineteenth century. The picture many of us have of children's health care often focuses on chronically ill children, spending long periods of time in drab hospital wards without their parents or friends. Playthings are also absent from this picture, and doctors and nurses are seen as stern-faced professionals, intent on the cure of the physical illness above all else. Within this picture there is little room for emotional care: the children's ward resembles the adult ward in everything but the size of the patients, and much of the photographic evidence which remains today suggests that the only warmth the children may have found would have come from the large cast-iron fireplace.

Even before 1850, however, there is evidence to show that health professionals recognised the detrimental effects of separation from parents. Indeed, Dr George Armstrong, the founder in 1769 of London's first dispensary for children (a type of outpatient facility which gave advice and medicines to the families of sick children on a charitable basis), was opposed to the admission of children to hospital because of this. Armstrong recognised that parents of the time would rarely be able to accompany a sick child into hospital and that ' "If you take a sick child away from the parents or nurse [i.e. nanny], you break its heart immediately" ' (Armstrong, 1767, cited by Miles, 1986).

By the 1850s a growing movement in Victorian Britain was of the opinion that hospital care for the children of the poor was of value, although separation remained an issue for some doctors. In 1850, in a response to Charles West's first appeal for funds to establish what was to become the Hospital for Sick Children at Great Ormond Street (GOS) the *Edinburgh Medical and Surgical Journal* of 1st April suggested that '. . . it will be well to make provisions in many instances for the reception of mothers with their children' (Kosky, 1989, p. 151). The early children's hospitals did not make such provision, however, possibly because the families of those children likely to be admitted were in similar circumstances to those known to Armstrong 80 years earlier. This is not to suggest that loss of contact with family and friends was not believed to be important, but rather that the benefits of hospital care were seen as ultimately over-riding the emotional problems caused by this separation.

Charles West, the physician who founded GOS in 1852, published the first textbook for sick children's nurses two years later. *How to Nurse Sick Children* (West, 1854) is addressed specifically to nurses at GOS with West describing himself as 'a person who has seen a great deal of little children, especially of little sick children, who loves them very much . . .' (p. 7). For West the love of children was a vital quality in anyone who wished to care for sick children. The 'special business' of the children's nurse 'when a child is ill, is to give it pleasure' (p. 62). West stresses the need to avoid causing 'needless distress and terror to little children' when giving nursing care (p. 63). This relatively brief book makes no overt reference to the care of a grieving child, but its overall tone suggests that emotional aspects of a child's care are recognised as important. The separation of the child from the family seems to be accepted as a necessity, a lesser evil when attempting to care for the sick children of the poor:

> . . . because so many are sick; because they languish in their homes; a burden to their parents who have no leisure to tend them, no means to minister to their wants. The one sick child weighs down the whole family; it keeps the father poor, the home wretched. The little one lives on in sadness, and dies in sorrow; a sorrow broken only by a strange gladness which even the mother can scarcely repress when the burden is removed, and the sick child is taken where it will be sick no more (West, 1854, p. 4)

West's perspective on the nursing care of sick children appears to have held its influence on at least some of the medical profession for some time. The American doctors who co-wrote *Virtue's Household Physician*, a textbook aimed at the lay reader first published in 1905, quote large sections of West's earlier work (without credit) in their section on 'How to Nurse Sick Children' (Buffum *et al.*, 1905, p. 492ff). Here again, the need of a sick child for love and care is stressed. So, too, is West's reminder that the nursing of sick children requires special qualities, for 'it is hard for the nurse to remember that sickness does not destroy the little loving heart, but only hides its affection for a short time' (p. 492).

Children's Nursing (Seymour Yapp, 1924) is an early example of a children's nursing textbook written by a nurse. Here again the need to meet the child's emotional needs is readily apparent. The Preface, for example, by J. Dudgeon Giles MD, refers to 'the need for that human kindliness and "mothering" which are the essential accompaniments of every detail in the successful nursing of children.' The importance of a love for children as a quality of the children's nurse is again emphasised.

Miss Seymour Yapp concentrates on practical nursing tasks, and separate sections on psychological care or the care of the grieving child are absent. But throughout the text numerous references are made which make it clear that such aspects of care were considered of vital importance. No mention is made of the benefits of having resident parents, but the child's grief after visiting time is identified and the nurse is advised to accept happily 'the passionate embrace of the child with hungry heart'.

The maintenance of a child's self-respect, the importance of play for the sick child and the involvement of the mother in the care of her dying child are all seen as vital in successful children's nursing. Interestingly, the book includes sections on care of children at home and on health visiting: this integrated perspective on care comes not from one of the specialist children's hospitals, but from the matron of a Poor Law Infirmary.

In much of child health care, however, the emotional needs of children appear to have been given little importance in the inter-war years. Urwin and Sharland (1992) suggest that parental love was given little emphasis by the child care literature of this period, although it had been of importance in previous years, and would be so again as new evidence regarding the emotional needs of children was revealed.

By the late 1940s the debate about the separation of children and families was returning to the idea that psychological and emotional care was of importance. Bowlby's early work with 'juvenile delinquents' had suggested to him the emotional and psychological trauma which could arise in children when their normal family relationships were disturbed (Bowlby, 1946). In 1949 Doctor Mildred Creak was reported as stating that 'Short periods in hospital could produce profound disturbances [of behaviour]' (*BMJ*, 1949, p. 90). In the following year Professor N.B. Capon wrote that 'it is now generally agreed that insufficient attention has been given to the emotional development of children' (Capon, 1950, p. 866). The practice of admitting mothers with their children appears to have been common in New Zealand by this time (*Lancet*, 1948, p. 376), while Professor J.C. Spence had been advocating this practice (at least as a means of reducing cross-infection) since 1933 (Spence, 1933, p. 440).

A crucial condemnation of child care in hospital came from Professor Spence in his 1946 Charles West Lecture, published in the

BMJ (Spence, 1947). Spence's picture of a children's ward is a depressing one: a picture of a place where the child's emotional care is of far less importance than it had been in the children's hospitals of the nineteenth century. His description is, he claims, 'not far off the mark in many of our hospitals'. It is a description of an environment which is likelier to create and compound a sense of loss than it is to prevent such a feeling:

> The room is vast. It contains twenty beds, spaced along walls tiled by Doulton or painted chocolate and yellow. The roof is . . . terrifyingly remote to the eyes of a child who lies many hours gazing at it . . . The beds stink just a little. Near the bed is a contraption, half-chair and half locker, but it is beyond the reach of the child except by a contortion he cannot make so soon after his operation. He defeats this by concealing his personal treasures under his pillow until they are again put out of his reach. He solaces himself with comics or with paper and a scrubby pencil which he cannot sharpen.
>
> He dislikes the pallid immobile child in the next bed because he is too young for companionship and too ill for talk, but, as is the way of children, he makes the best of it, and carries on a conversation with a boy of his own age ten yards away over the heads of a whimpering baby and a plaintive 2-year-old standing behind the bars of his cot clad in a shapeless nightgown with a loose napkin sunk to his ankles below. . . . Night comes on, but there is no bedtime story, no last moment of intimacy, no friendly cuddle before sleep. The nurse is too busy for that . . .
>
> In the hospital there are other wards like this, with a kitchen, a side-room, a linen cupboard, and an entrance corridor beyond which parents shall not pass. They have no treatment room, no laboratory, no accommodation for parents, no interviewing room . . .
>
> Not all hospitals are like this. Some are better, but many are worse (Spence, 1947, p. 127–128).

By the early 1950s the modern view of separation and its possible ill-effects on the child was becoming defined. A key element in this definition was a 45-minute black-and-white film, produced by James Robertson in 1951–1952 in order to inform a wide audience of child health professionals about the lack of psychological care on offer to children. 'A Two-year-old Goes to Hospital' followed Laura through her eight-day stay on a children's ward in an unnamed hospital. Admitted for routine surgery to repair an umbilical hernia, Laura's physical treatment and recovery appear uneventful. Her emotional care, as described by Robertson, is far less successful.

Fig. 1.1 Christmas on a children's ward, c. 1947. A happy scene, with an abundance of toys and games. But relatives are notably absent.

Laura appears to spend most of her time alone (Fig. 1.2), as do the rest of the children. The ward appears stark and clinical, with no obvious child-oriented decoration and few toys or books. Even the brief period of play which Laura has with a nurse each day is, according to the narration, not part of normal routine.

Laura seems to be from a stable, caring and secure family setting. The health problem causing her admission is a minor one and the treatment is routine and uneventful. Her mother visits whenever ward policy allows (for brief periods in the afternoon) and father also visits on one or two occasions. Laura is unlikely to have been viewed as suffering from a major loss: but her grief is clearly recognisable to the modern child care professional.

From his work with Laura and others, Robertson developed a three-stage model to describe the responses to the grief of separation demonstrated by young children: Protest, Despair and Denial/Detachment (Robertson and Robertson, 1989, p. 14). This classification of the stages of grief remains of relevance today, and forms part of the foundation of child health professionals' knowledge.

By the early 1960s the modern ideals of children's nursing were becoming more overt. Winifred Hector's *Modern Nursing: Theory*

Fig. 1.2 Laura, alone on the ward. (From the film 'A Two-year-old Goes to Hospital' by James Robertson. Reproduced by kind permission of Joyce Robertson.)

and Practice, in its second edition of 1962, was clear about the sense of loss occasioned in children by separating them from their families. Daily visiting is indicated as the norm, while admitting the mother along with her child is also suggested, with the mother continuing to care for her child as much as possible. The importance of other family members in a child's life is mentioned, while the role of the father also receives consideration: 'Since toddlers have fathers as well as mothers, the male nurse can also play an important part in their management.' While Bowlby and other researchers are not mentioned by Hector, this is clearly a text which shows their influence on ideas about loss and grief.

Nursing textbooks in the 1990s, whether or not aimed specifically at child care nurses, all accept the need to minimise the effects of separation. Family-centred care is taken as the norm, with the psychological aspects of care given emphasis on a par with physical care. The fear of separating child and family is enshrined in Government publications, which see hospitalisation as a 'last resort' (Department of Health, 1991) and extends across social and welfare services, where the removal of a child from parental care is also a last-resort strategy.

The recognition of separation as a source of grief for children, whether that separation is occasioned by hospitalisation or for another reason, is a fundamental aspect of the orthodoxy of child health care. The current emphasis on family-centred care, the return to community health care of children with hospitalisation as a 'last resort' and the increasing professionalisation of care for grieving children are all responses, directly or indirectly, to Robertson and Bowlby's work, however belated some of these responses have been.

Reconstructing Childhood and Responses to Children's Grief

In the last 150 years, children's lives, child health care and our recognition of, and responses to, children's grief have undergone major changes. In some cases these changes have been gradual: responses to social changes which have affected all aspects of childhood. In other cases, such as our awareness of the psychological effects of hospitalisation, they have been relatively swift, brought about by research findings which have quickly gained widespread acceptance. It is important to remember that these changes have not always moved child health care in one direction. There is growing evidence to suggest that the psychological care of children actually lost its early importance for many child health professionals during the first half of the twentieth century before gaining its current pre-eminence.

It is also important to remember that our current ideas regarding children's grief are not the end point of these years of development; rather they are the current orthodoxy, open themselves to change resulting from new research or new social perspectives on children and childhood. Indeed, it may well be that we are once again entering a crucial period for the reconstruction of our ideas of 'childhood' and that our approaches to children's loss and grief will as a result undergo a major shift in focus. Whether or not this is the case, working with children in situations of loss is a vital and demanding function. It is one which should be informed by an understanding of its own history, while also striving to develop its own future.

References

Aries, P. (1973) *Centuries of Childhood*. Harmondsworth: Penguin.

Bowlby, J. (1946) *Forty-four Juvenile Thieves: their characters and home life*. London: Baillière, Tindall & Cox.

Bowlby, J. (1969) *Attachment and Loss. Volume 1: Attachment*. London: Hogarth Press.

British Medical Journal (1949) **II**:90.

Buffum, H.E., Warren, I., Thorndike, W., Lovering, A.T., Small, A.E., Heber Smith, J. (1905) *Virtue's Household Physician. A twentieth century medica*. London: Virtue and Company.

Capon, N.B. (1950) Development and behaviour of children. *British Medical Journal*, **I**: 859–869.

Davin, A. (1978) Imperialism and Motherhood. *History Workshop*, **5**: 9–65.

Department of Health (1991) *Welfare of Children and Young People in Hospital*. London: HMSO.

Hector, W. (1962) *Modern Nursing: Theory and Practice*. London: William Heinemann.

Hendrick, H. (1990) Constructions and Reconstructions of British Childhood: An Interpretative Survey, 1800 to the Present. In A. James and A. Prout (Eds), *Constructing and Reconstructing Childhood: Contemporary Issues in the Sociological Study of Childhood*. London: Falmer Press.

Heywood, J.S. (1969) *Childhood and Society a Hundred Years Ago*. London: National Children's Home.

Kosky, J. (1989) *Mutual Friends: Charles Dickens and Great Ormond Street Children's Hospital*. London: Weidenfeld and Nicolson.

Lancet (1948) **I**: 376.

Miles, I. (1986) The emergence of sick children's nursing Part 1 Sick children's nursing before the turn of the century. *Nurse Education Today* **6**: 82–87.

Ministry of Education (1947) *The Health of the School Child. Report of the Chief Medical Officer of the Ministry of Education for the Years 1939–1945.* London: HMSO.

Phillips, T. (1994) Children and Power. In B. Lindsay (Ed.) *The Child and Family: contemporary nursing issues in child health and care.* London: Baillière Tindall.

Robertson, J. and Robertson, J. (1989) *Separation and the Very Young.* London: Free Association Books.

Rose, L. (1990) *The Erosion of Childhood. Child Oppression in Britain 1860–1918.* London: Routledge.

Seymour Yapp, C. (1924) *Children's Nursing. Lectures to Probationers.* London: Poor Law Publications.

Spence, J.C. (1933) Control of Infection (Letter) *Lancet* **I**: 440.

Spence, J.C. (1947) The care of children in hospital. *British Medical Journal* **1**: 125.

Urwin, C. and Sharland, E. (1992) From bodies to minds in childcare literature. Advice to parents in inter-war Britain. In R. Cooter (ed.), *In the Name of the Child. Health and Welfare, 1880–1940.* London: Routledge.

West, C. (1854) *How to Nurse Sick Children.* London: Longman, Brown, Green and Longmans.

White, Franklin A. (1964) Children's hospitals. In F.N.L. Poynter (Ed.), *The Evolution of Hospitals in Britain.* London: Pitman Medical.

2
Developmental Perspectives

Betty Rathbone

Individuals are learning about their world and being influenced by it even before they emerge from the womb. They have also marked differences one from another and mothers can tell when they are carrying a child with a particularly active or passive nature. All throughout childhood there will be interactions between the child's unique makeup, driven by genetic endowment, and the experiences that support or damage unfolding potential. Early attempts to separate out what is caused by 'heredity' from what is due to 'environment' could seldom give specific and definite answers, especially about the fate of an individual. Most of what will be said about what can be expected of children at various ages and stages of development is subject to exceptions. There is never any substitute for careful observation or being prepared to listen.

Throughout the process of change and development children need the reassuring influence of special people in their lives on whom they can rely for resolution of any crisis. The influence of these attachment figures on the success with which children adjust to the losses they encounter is considerable. Attachment figures are of central importance and their significance is discussed before outlining the ways in which children are likely to handle loss and grief at different stages in their development.

Principles of Attachment

Bowlby's classic books on attachment are the basis of current knowledge (Bowlby, 1969, 1973, 1980). The key element of the theory is the need for human beings to have special people in their lives on whom they can rely for resolution of any crisis. Part of our propensity to learn is devoted to sorting out who can be trusted to be there for us when needed, particularly when the need is a social or emotional one.

Attachment is most commonly to the mother but happens with others too. The child who has a warm father or granny who plays and is affectionate, and a mother who is cold, albeit very efficient at dealing with physical needs, will very likely not have the mother as the primary attachment figure. Dunn (1993) found that siblings who have unresponsive mothers may become more attached to each other than those who have warmer parents. So that it seems the child will form the bond with the best available person – who may be the family dog. Children who have formed bonds to more than one person generally are not equally attached and will show who is the key figure by their behaviour when ill or otherwise exceptionally threatened, since they revert to basics in these situations and want to be near their most important person. Some children develop attachments to 'transitional objects' which serve to symbolise the attainability of comfort in distress. For a child in grief, the discovery or rediscovery of such an object may be very helpful. However, not all children use this mechanism and some do not choose the cuddly teddy bear or piece of old towel. It is worth remembering that smell is a primitive sense and important in primitive emotional attachments; the newly washed cuddly is not as good as the one that smells of mother. A mother will do well to leave a treasured object with her child in order to help offset the sense of being abandoned.

Attachment figures who are not happy and confident in their world, for example those who are chronically depressed or suffering acute bereavement reactions, may set up unhelpful 'insecure attachments' in those dependent on them. The basic tendency to seek comfort – to reduce anxiety – brings the child closer to the adult. This is a primitive survival mechanism; immature animals are more likely to fall victim to predators if on their own. This mechanism goes wrong when the adult is neglectful, dangerous, or anxiety ridden. Proximity is apt to produce more distress and so the child becomes aloof, at the extreme showing 'frozen watchfulness' and having no energy to spare for normal activity and learning. Less drastically, there may be a slowing or a block in emotional development so that the capacity for more mature relationships is impaired and the person continues to react to situations in immature ways.

The loss of an attachment figure, for whatever reason, can have a profound effect on a child. The risk of these children developing depression in later life is considerably increased, especially when poverty compounds other reasons for anxiety and insecurity (Tweed *et al.*, 1989; Matson, 1989). When it is an important attachment figure who is lost to the child there is a need for a replacement. However, unless the process of grieving is completed there will not be the necessary detachment from the original love and attempts to be or provide a substitute will fail.

Age-related Capacities for Adjustment

First two years: infant and toddler

It is sometimes supposed that pre-verbal children do not need as much nursing through a bereavement as an older child or adult who can understand and talk about what has happened, but there is documented association of heightened risk of mental illness, depression and antisocial behaviour in individuals who have suffered the early loss of one or other parent (McKnew *et al.*, 1985).

Infants from the first weeks pay more attention to mother's face or mother's voice than to another similar woman; there is no such thing as a baby who is too young to appreciate the difference in carers. Overt fear when a strange person has dealings with a baby generally appears around eight months and insistence on being in at least visual contact with the attachment figure tends to be at its height around eighteen months, in the course of normal development.

If the child is not given good responsive care in the early months there is a failure in the establishment of basic trust. This failure will colour what goes on in later development, both in intellectual and emotional terms. Spitz (in Bowlby, 1969) documents a high casualty rate in infants in orphanages; infants become listless, sometimes die, and sometimes show severe mental retardation, which could only be partially reversed by later improved care. These infants were given food and kept clean but had nothing to look at, and nurses were not allowed to have special relationships with any child. Thus these infants had no personal security, no opportunity to get stimulation by handling objects, and no chances to be effective in producing change in their world. Deprivation of both security and stimulus needs applied, and had drastic results.

First six months

Discomfort may result if the child is too hot or too cold; hunger is devastating, and so is the colic that goes with getting the wrong food at the wrong time. Ill infants have been shown to respond well to water beds, being laid on lambs' wool, and being kept kangaroo fashion in skin-to-skin contact with mother, highlighting the importance of touch sensations to well-being. Later, in favourable conditions there is a developing ability to self-regulate temperature, to produce sensations by moving themselves and their toys about, and to predict events. Frequent changes of carer and of regime, as may happen with difficulties in finding childminders, can interfere with this process. The use of routine, the predictability of things, and people coming to respond soon after need is felt helps the child to get through the phase where crying is the main means of communication. In the early months, quick response to crying, followed by effective action, helps to produce the older child who does not cry and winge and is able to develop better ways of expressing needs and to tolerate having to wait for a short time.

Six months onwards

The relative importance of physical and social factors changes as children develop. Whereas several people may be able to meet the child's earlier physical and stimulus needs, the older infant and toddler need stable attachment figures who can be relied on to help the world be a safe place to explore. As well as learning to wait for wants to be supplied, the crawler and toddler must learn about the limits of acceptable exploration. Consistent rules, applied in a firm and loving fashion, will lay the first foundations for an acceptance of limits to personal freedom (Herbert, 1991). The child who is mainly cared for by a depressed adult (as may be the case if the attachment figure is still grieving over the loss of a partner or parent of their own) is liable to miss out on healthy exploration. These children risk staying too close and learning to be too fearful of the world or becoming antisocial because exploration does not have any limits and there is no adult to share exciting discoveries. There may be physical risk of accidents which can result in death or long-term disability, but the emotional risks are as serious.

Pre-school children

The setting of standards for personal behaviour and the beginning of a sense of personal autonomy are often linked with toilet training. Neural maturation occurs earlier for the bowel than the bladder. Thus a 'clean' child may not be able to manage to be 'dry' as well. Carers who are sensitive can find the time when the child is able to manage, and so make this milestone a very positive one. Repeated failure, criticism and anger are associated with unfavourable personality development. A child who is emotionally upset and or in strange surroundings is more likely to have accidents and to suffer shame afterwards. Insecurity will be compounded by punishment and long-term elimination problems are a possible consequence (Saul, 1979).

At any age, children are likely to lose their most recent skills under stress, and yet also to be ready to be taught how to cope with a new situation. With support, the regressive tendencies can be short lived and the thrust to maturity the main coping mechanism. Pre-school children will try to comfort and help where they perceive distress and will have a notion of being good as a way of making things better. They have started to use language to communicate and ask questions. These questions sometimes seem to demand answers to spiritual issues (Crompton, 1992). The question 'Where is . . . ?' in regard to a dead person can be answered on two levels and the child needs to have the concrete level sorted out before answers about spiritual matters are attempted. An understanding of what has happened to the body and why it has to be disposed of needs to underpin the dialogue about beliefs concerning the fate of the consciousness or the soul.

When both parents are alive, but no longer live together and there is no contact with the non-custodial parent, there are loyalty issues in addition to the grief associated with the loss of a relationship. Apparent forgetting of a key attachment figure who disappears may cover issues that will surface later in life. Atkin and Rubin (1976) give useful guidelines for the divorced father who wishes to do well by his children. Even so, the evidence of a follow-up study by Allison and Furstenberg (1989) is that young children are especially vulnerable to divorce, as manifest in problem behaviour, psychological distress and academic performance, and the impact is not related to whether the custodial parent remarries or whether there are siblings.

Persistent use of 'Why?' is characteristic of children who are in the early stages of mastering language, and having a familiar story repeated over and over again is also age appropriate. Children use stories to make sense of their world and what would be boring repetition to an older child or an adult is part of the process of intellectual development which comes before formal learning. Early spoken language is facilitated by repetition of jingles, nursery rhymes or advertisements, and these help mastery of sentence structure. Using simple sentences to a child who still uses single words to share experience helps bring about grammatical speech. The rate of learning new words is very rapid in pre-school children; they should be given the correct words to describe the experiences they are having and especially helped to label their feelings and to recognise those feelings in others. One of the strengths of the Thomas The Tank Engine books is talk of feelings the children know in themselves; fear, guilt, sadness, laziness, envy, can be dealt with and forgiven. Children do not have to know that the Fat Controller is taking the reassuring parental role or that they identify with one of the engines (though they may well have a favourite engine, the one that seems most like them). Magical thinking is natural, so that pre-school children like stories about animals and machinery that suffer losses similar to the real life events that need to be dealt with.

Playthings support the need for repetition which is strong in pre-school children. They may need lots of tries to master the sequence of events for an operation or a funeral. Given dolls, miniatures of real objects, clay, painting and drawing materials, they will work towards mastery of trauma and construction of a viable story. The adult who lets the child pace play (but who is there to find suitable tools for the job the child wants to do) may in extreme instances be a highly trained and skilled professional therapist, but usually the naturally available people and resources will be 'good enough'.

Denial that the worst could have happened, 'My Mummy is *not* going to have to spend her life in a wheelchair' and avoiding the fact by focusing on everything else that has changed, 'My Mummy does not do it like that' is likely to be repetitive, just like any other learning activity, and can lead to conflict with carers. The temptation to deny, and the hope that the loved figure may be found after all, appear early in development and remain characteristic of the first stages of bereavement reaction at any age. Similarly, there is a risk that later loss, even breaking an object or mislaying a toy, may produce grief which connects with the main loss and so seems to produce an unreasonable degree of upset. Such outbursts may offer a chance to talk about the real trauma, which is worth taking as normal defences are down. Trying to get through defences at other times can vary from slow and difficult to impossible. Magical thinking can lead a child to feel enormous misplaced guilt and to devise a story with lasting negative consequences, especially if adults are being punitive about lapses from expected standards, or insisting that the child be kept ignorant.

As school age is approached, it becomes more important that a child has opportunity to meet peers and to build up a sense of personal autonomy. Going out to playgroup or nursery satisfies both stimulation and social needs, although after a loss the child may want to have a familiar figure to stay around until basic security is re-established.

Primary school children: 5–10 years

The move to school is a big milestone and goes with increasing demands on the child to be self-reliant.

The first teacher makes a big impression and gives the skills that will be crucial in successful learning. Self-esteem is a critical factor in school achievement (Purkey, 1986). Settled children develop an appetite for facts, often channelled into a particular area of interest, maybe football teams or the latest heroes on television. On the whole these facts are amassed rather than reasoned about and children continue to live mainly in the present, although they begin to learn about happenings which are in the past or beyond their direct experience. Play continues to be an important part of life and can be the enemy of adults who have to keep children moving to the demands of the clock and the school syllabus rather than letting them follow their own interests. Stamina may hardly be up to demands on energy, so that it is not uncommon for children to have many illnesses which interrupt school attendance, especially early on. Stress will depress the resistance to infection further, so that the children with most need to learn may be away most often and start to despair of mastering academic learning.

If the stresses of life events cause a child to fall behind in learning, it is important to give help before the problem becomes one of self-esteem as well as lack of skill. A sense of mastery of new skills is therapeutic at any age but particularly at this stage of development (see Erikson in Smith and Cowie, 1991). Tantrums easily arise from ambitions that outrun skills, and help is needed from adults if projects are to be seen through and not abandoned half way. The process of making can be more important than the product, but it may matter to the child that adults treasure what they have produced. It is safer to treasure what the child has finished with than to throw away something that turns out to have had symbolic value. Children in this age group thrive on limited responsibility, especially in traumatic circumstances, but they also need time and space to be with peers and to imagine themselves in various non-real situations.

Physical growth is steadier than in pre-school years and activity is an important part of self-expression. Children who are extra restless and reckless (who might be classified as suffering from Attention Deficit Hyperactive Disorder) are more likely to have accidents resulting in broken limbs, and even suffer spinal injuries that put them in wheelchairs. Children with muscular dystrophy are losing strength and skill just when their peers are branching out. Both these groups are high risk for emotional disturbance in addition to their underlying problem.

Boys and girls will be more or less stereotyped by gender, according to the customs of the group where they grow up, and will be very aware of what their roles are supposed to be. A child who is not able to be 'a real boy' or 'a nice girl' or 'the right type for this school' will suffer. Prejudices about race and class begin to bite. The child who is getting to look increasingly like a lost parent may experience severe pressure in the form of expectations of similar behaviour.

A child's experience might be one of never being able to reach an idealised standard, or of behaviour being seen as 'bad traits' that fit old memories. Either way, freedom to be a new person in new circumstances is being restricted by a family or neighbourhood myth, and depression or rebellion are likely. The effort to be a perfect child can succeed, in so far as presently pleasing adults is concerned, but this is a hollow adjustment and a very poor foundation for the later demands of adolescent development.

A child who is aware that there may be no chance to experience youth and later ages, because of a life threatening illness, is more likely to think deeply about the meaning of life and to need to share ideas about this than one who is sheltered. Do not assume that a child in exceptional circumstances is 'too young for serious talk'. If an offered chance to ask questions about what is going on produces a lot of interest in technical gadgets, then communication needs to be conducted at this level; if it produces existential questions, then these deserve an honest sharing.

Encouragement to be creative by writing poetry, drawing,

painting or making clay shapes is particularly relevant when every-one is having problems in expression. Ability to create develops from imitation. In normal or abnormal circumstances children benefit from experience of music, poetry and drama, which touch on things they know about and then branch out in new and exciting ways.

Early adolescence: 11–13 years

The rapid physical changes that go with puberty are the next developmental challenge and a period of great self-consciousness and doubt about attractiveness is likely to occur. This time is easier for those who mature at an average rate, but still demands the radical change in self- image that goes with losing a child's body. Early maturers may seem to be more able to cope than they actually are, whereas late maturers have the anxiety of trying to keep up with much stronger and taller peers and of worrying if they will ever have an acceptable adult physique. The opinion of peers is very important and focus of interests is still in the here and now rather than looking to the future. Friendships are a very important part of life, and experiments in relationships with different kinds of people may cause friction at home. Loss of a 'best friend' associated with a move of school occasioned by job changes for a parent may be a major blow to a child who is not easily able to find new friends in a new environment. If a parent has gone to prison, the social stigma can be especially hard to bear at this stage.

There is a shift towards more abstract and systematic thinking, although not yet an adult ability to order and systematise what is known and to reason with complete logic. Although younger chil-dren already have the capacity to understand rules of behaviour and to talk about right and wrong in terms of what makes people happy or sad, talk of being good at a more abstract level is more likely at this stage (see Kohlberg in Smith and Cowie, 1991).

An ideal of how things should be leads to comparisons with the actual life being experienced, which can be a source of extra pain for those who have poor experiences. The contrast between what rich people have and what poor people can afford may hit someone in this age group very hard if their life circumstances include a sudden drop in the standard of living. Shame at not having the current status symbols of the age group and anger at the new restrictions on activities are felt especially keenly and compound the grief reactions to bereavement or divorce or moving to a poorer neighbourhood following parental loss of employment.

Whereas older children often seem to have achieved a mastery of their emotions and to be full of common sense about everyday demands by the end of the primary school years, the onset of adolescence produces new demands. Rapid growth is tiring and so is the change from primary to secondary education. 'Laziness' is more likely to be an issue as more is expected of adolescents who are feeling unsure of where they fit in and who swing between being children and being adult oriented. The pressures of trauma can swing a young adolescent back into childishness or up into an apparent ability to function in an adult helping role. Neither extreme is a healthy place to be stuck. Drama is a useful way of exploring feelings, role play allowing for release from a stuck position without the need to have the problem spelt out in a way that feels humiliating to a self-conscious adolescent. An attempt to be hectically involved in every activity going or to play constant loud music are other ways of getting extra stimulation to numb pain. The anger that goes with loss easily translates into complaints and rudeness to would-be helpful adults, much as happens with young children, but with the added force that comes from more years of learning. The temptation to ease the situation by conceding every demand is great, especially if there has already been a habit of using gifts as a substitute for the effort of sharing feelings and trying to work out a family event. Group work needs a strong leader who can contain what is released rather than have everyone overwhelmed and further traumatised, and is very useful as a natural forum for learning and asking questions that may be hard or impossible for the family to answer.

Later adolescence: 14 and above

The main life task is still the forming of a personal identity but, once the growth spurt at puberty has past and hopefully the individual has accepted the form of the adult body, there is more of an orientation to the adult world. Previously careless scholars start to behave better and to find personal ambitions that are worth working for in the adult world. The ability to reason logically becomes much more reliable in ordinary circumstances and challenges to adult authority are offered from a position of felt equality – which may or may not be acceptable to the family who still hope to be relating on an authoritarian basis. In favourable circumstances the skills of negotiation are learned through the regular revision of levels of responsibility and freedom appropriate to developing skill and maturity.

Previous incomplete success in life tasks increases the difficulty of accomplishing the next stage of maturing. It can easily be the case that someone in this age group is still struggling with earlier issues and is not able to fulfill current expectations. If earlier failure in nurturing has been extreme, perhaps because of chronically ill or absent parents, there is a risk of a rush towards leaving home before having the skills for survival in the adult world. Similarly, a sexual partner can be chosen and a 'home' set up by people who both hope for far more than the chosen partner can deliver. This premature restarting of the family cycle then sets the scene for another child to have a poor start, unless enough outside support is given to alter the cycle of deprivation (Anthony and Cohler, 1987). Failure to pass exams at the level required to further keenly held ambitions, or even the fear of such failure, is major pressure and suicide attempts, successful or otherwise, are associated with academic and vocational hazards.

The risk of substance abuse begins before this age, partly because children like to copy adult behaviour they see in their lives or on television and video. Primary school children are more likely to follow healthy living advice than adolescents, but regular smokers in adolescence often start before that. Smoking as a response to stress is particularly common in adolescent girls and is likely to be a group activity which is resistant to attempts by adults to stop it (Gust *et al.*, 1988). Drinking excess alcohol, sniffing glue, or taking illegal drugs are more likely to be obvious in teenage years. These habits easily pass from occasional experiments to get extra stimulation to being the main activity in life, especially if there are reasons to be depressed and a need to try to stifle pain. If life seems too difficult anyway, active or passive attempts to end it will not be stopped by adults pointing out that later health will be impaired. All forms of self-harm, including eating disorders, self-inflicted injury and overdoses with or without real risk to life, go with an inability to confront existential issues, and measures that do not address these issues are unlikely to help for long (Patros and Shamoo, 1989).

Opportunities to revisit old traumas which are blocking development may arise during attempts to deal with more recent crises, so that counsellors will do well to allow scope for discussion of events that do not have obvious relevance in the present. For people who naturally think in pictures, contact between past, present and future through images may be a good way to unravel tangles. Interpretation in terms of Jungian or other theory may help in skilled hands (this is the particular expertise of the art therapist) but there can be considerable value in simply giving the youngster art materials and time and space to use them. There may be outpourings of poetry from those who are more comfortable with words and encouragement to write a narrative of events and feelings helps to externalise and come to terms with difficulties. Music making, both formal and informal, is another outlet which is available and useful to younger children as well but is particularly useful to older adolescents who are more skillful and able to vary the means of expression. Involvement in staging a musical or dramatic performance satisfies many kinds of needs and is most satisfying for those who can work along with enthusiastic adults who can use and teach skills and mitigate deficiencies.

Moral issues are apt to matter a great deal and the search for the right codes to live by can be particularly difficult for those who have a home culture which is at odds with that of the majority of their peers. Issues of race and class can go with persecution of the person who is in the minority. Bullying, both physical and emotional, can make life intolerable and it is sometimes unleashed in more virulent form when the victim suffers some other misfortune. Much remains hidden, either because of shame or because of realistic fears that telling ineffectual adults will be useless or worse. Unlike younger children who are quite likely not to notice that adults are imperfect, adolescents may experience deep disillusion when sexual or financial habits are clearly not those prescribed by the rules. A father who causes injury by driving when drunk may be defended against others' criticisms but also be a shattering disappointment to the adolescent in the family.

Key Points

- Understanding, whether of language, pictures or complex human situations, is typically ahead of the individual's ability to express what they think is happening. It never pays to patronise.

- Trust is basic in development of relationships and the earliest experiences continue to colour the way a child copes. Do not take it as a personal insult if suspicion of you and your motives is an early reaction in the traumatised child, and be ready for pessimism to crop up over all sorts of issues.

- When in doubt, look for an activity that this person is known to enjoy and share it with them.

- Play is a fundamental activity for mastery of the world and particularly important when there is a big adjustment to be made. 'I wish I could fly', (Maris, 1986) is a book written on this theme for 4–6 year olds. The hero turtle comes in to his own when it rains, after being helpless and worse than his friends at other activities. Many traditional fairy stories about the despised or neglected child who finally succeeds appeal to the same dynamic and can help children believe in their ability to succeed in spite of adversity. Real-life accounts of similarly situated individuals who have overcome difficulties can be useful with the older child.

- People do not develop in isolation and therefore if we want to understand how a given event is going to affect a child we must pay attention to both the fine detail of his or her experience of the day and to what has happened in this child's past. For someone who is already sensitised by tragedy, a cold fact finding can be experienced as additional trauma, even though the interviewer is literally 'just trying to understand'. It can be worse when there is a question of later legal proceedings and the interviewer has preparation of a case in mind. This is most likely to happen where sexual abuse is in question but it can also be true when traffic or other accidents that may give cause for legal liability are being investigated. Mitchels and Prince (1992) offer a guide to good practice in these circumstances.

- The child's questions matter most. Remembering that intellectual development feeds on information and that children can make more use of answers to questions that they have thought of than to questions that belong to adult concerns is important. Even when the priority is to get information from children, it pays to ask what puzzles them rather than to try to clarify their thoughts by giving forced choices. When words are difficult, pictures may do better in getting a dialogue going. For someone who is physically active and restless, talking is easier when not sat still.

- Answer questions in simple form first and be seen to be ready to answer more, up to the point where the discussion is elaborate enough to satisfy the questioner. If you don't understand what the child's question means try rephrasing it and asking if you have it right. Offer a concrete interpretation first, for example, a response to the question 'Where is mummy?' could be 'Do you mean where in the cemetery?' to which the child might reply 'Daddy said she is in Heaven.'

- Be prepared to talk about spiritual questions even with young children – if they can ask the question they are starting to be able to think of answers. It is always important to know how a family culture looks at questions the child is asking – in the moral and spiritual area it is crucial. There may be an adolescent rebellion against a family faith or an attempt to stay with a minority view against the pressure from peers of differing faiths or none. An acknowledgement that people need to keep coming back to look at these questions as they go through different life stages may give enough common ground between family, child and carer, for stumbling blocks to development to be removed.

- Allow for unevenness in coping; the same person may need holding like a baby, hearing a simple story with a moral like a pre-schooler, playing with images on paper or with clay like a school child, long conversations with peers like a young adolescent, a serious look at new life choices like an older adolescent, and to talk about unanswerable questions like any human being.

- Resilience feeds on the experience of success in solving manageable bits of the problems posed in a difficult life. The companion questions 'What can I do about it?' and 'What can you do about it?' begin to address the situation in ways that help to prevent the learned helplessness which is at the root of much long term depression (Williams, 1988). It is all the more important to find small but symbolically important answers so that there is an 'I can' in the present and an 'I did' as part of the eventual story of past events.

Conclusion

Loss can pose a significant threat to a child's well-being and development. Children who are confronted with massive loss are massively at risk. Research on those who cope, the resilient, shows, as usual, some factors to do with experience and some inborn. Those who were cheerful infants, easy to get in to a routine, not fearful of strange situations or new people, have a flying start over the ones who as babies were easily startled, shy of new situations and not good at amusing themselves. Those who beat the odds after a difficult start have commonly had one key person in their lives who kept a consistent interest in their well-being, maybe a teacher or a family friend. They have been given tasks within their capabilities which they believed helped to make things better and have been given generous appreciation for what they have contributed

(Greenspan, 1995; Salk, 1992; Robins and Rutter, 1990). If carers can build pride in being a survivor and determination to help prevent suffering for others who might be in similar circumstances, that is a giant therapeutic step.

References

Allison, P. and Furstenberg, F.F. (1989) How marital dissolution affects children: variations by age and sex. *Developmental Psychology*, **25**: 540.

Anthony, E.J. and Cohler, J.C. (Eds) (1987) *The Invulnerable Child*. New York: The Guilford Press.

Atkin, E. and Rubin, E. (1976) *Part Time Father*. Vanguard Press: New York.

Bowlby, J. (1969) *Attachment and Loss, Volume 1: Attachment*. New York: Basic Books.

Bowlby, J. (1973) *Attachment and Loss, Volume 2: Separation, Anxiety and Anger*. London: Hogarth.

Bowlby, J. (1980) *Attachment and Loss, Volume 3: Loss: Sadness and Depression*. London: Hogarth.

Crompton, M. (1992) *Children and Counselling*. London: Edward Arnold.

Dunn, J. (1993) *Young Children's Close Relationships*. London: Sage.

Greenspan, S. (1995) Bonding with your child is vital and rewarding. *Child and Adolescent Behaviour Newsletter*, **11**: 8.

Gust, T. *et al.* (1988) Prevalence of tobacco dependence and withdrawal. *American Journal of Psychiatry*, **114**: 204.

Herbert, M. (1991) *Clinical Child Psychology*. Chichester: John Wiley.

Maris, R. (1986) *I Wish I Could Fly*. London: MacRae.

Matson, J.I. (1989) *Treating Depression in Children and Adolescents*. New York: Pergamon.

McKnew, D.H. *et al.* (1985) *Why Isn't Johnny Crying? Coping With Depression in Children*. New York: W.W. Norton.

Mitchels, B. and Prince, A. (1992) *The Children Act and Medical Practice*. Bristol: Family Law.

Patros, P.G. and Shamoo, T.K. (1989) *Depression and Suicide in Children and Adolescents: Prevention, Intervention and Postvention*. Boston: Alleyn and Bacon.

Purkey, W.W. (1986) *Self Concept and School Achievement*. Englewood Cliffs NJ: Prentice Hall.

Robins, L. and Rutter, M. (Eds) (1990) *Straight and Devious pathways from Childhood to Adulthood*. Cambridge: Cambridge University Press.

Salk, L. (1992) *Familyhood: Nurturing the Values that Matter*. New York: Simon and Schuster.

Saul, L.J. (1979) *Childhood Emotional Pattern: Key to Personality, its Disorders and Therapy*. New York: Van Nostrand Reinhold.

Smith, P.K. and Cowie, H. (1991) *Understanding Children's Development*, 2nd edn. London: Blackwell.

Tweed, J.L. *et al.* (1989) The effects of childhood parental death and divorce on six month history of anxiety disorders. *British Journal of Psychiatry*, **154**: 823.

Williams, J.M.G. *et al.* (1988) *Cognitive Psychology and Emotional Disorders*. Chichester: John Wiley.

3
Breaking Bad News To Children

John Elsegood

There is no one right way to break bad news but some ways are more helpful than others. The suggestions presented in this chapter do not provide an infallible formula for getting it right – there is no such thing. Nor are they based on any assumption that children should be told. But, if one of the reasons for not telling a child is that the adults involved do not know of a helpful way of going about it, then this chapter will help. Each situation is different and the bearer of bad news should always respond to the needs of the child rather than persist with a predetermined plan if it becomes no longer appropriate. However, the principles presented do provide a much needed set of beacons from which the person disclosing bad news can take bearings and so head in the *right direction,* as he or she travels *with the child* along a *unique* path and one that will be *ever changing* as they react to the unfolding news and respond to each other. These principles can be applied to any situation involving the disclosure of bad news to children.

Parents and professional carers are on the front line in situations involving breaking bad news. Doctors, nurses, midwives, health visitors, speech therapists, physiotherapists, social workers, probation officers, counsellors, child and family therapists, ministers of religion and the staff of children's homes are some of the many professional carers who can become involved. However, anyone who is involved with children could be confronted with this difficulty: other members of the family, friends, neighbours, teachers, career advisers, police officers, childminders, playschool staff and leaders of clubs and organisations to which children belong.

Bad News

Bad news is any news that drastically alters for the worse the child's view of his or her past and/or future, or those of someone who is important to that child. Breaking bad news involves responding to the child's reaction as well as delivering the news. Whatever the situation, bad news always involves loss, and accepting the reality of the bad news marks the beginning of a grieving process. For those children who have known about or suspected the bad news before it is openly disclosed, this process may have already begun.

Situations involving breaking bad news to children are as numerous and varied as the losses which can be experienced by them. Bad news can be related to a variety of medical, social and domestic circumstances including: acute and chronic illness; disability; hospitalisation; death; divorce; starting a new school; moving to a new neighbourhood; school examination results and career interviews; competitions; adoption; going into foster care and changing foster parents; and separation from a parent who is in prison or who works abroad, or from a sibling who moves away from home. Bad news can be about situations which are temporary or permanent. Some causes of bad news can be acted on whereas others cannot. The news can be about what has happened or what is likely to happen and will often include at least some uncertainties. At times the bad news will be about the child who is being told, on other occasions it will be about someone who is important to that child.

Children are usually informed of bad news either as a proactive or a reactive disclosure. A proactive disclosure is one which is initiated by an adult. Children told in this way may have no inkling of what is about to be disclosed or they may already know or at least suspect that something is amiss. On the other hand a reactive disclosure is initiated by the child and the disclosure is made by an adult in response to a question or concern that the child has expressed. In a reactive disclosure the child almost invariably knows at least something about the bad news. Children are quick to recognise clues that suggest all is not well; even subtle changes in people's behaviour toward them and toward each other do not go undetected. Sometimes the information on which they base their deduction is more convincing and brutal: the sibling who reveals, 'Mummy and Daddy are getting divorced', or the friend who says, 'My Mum says you're going into hospital to die'.

Giving bad news is rarely confined to a single telling and usually involves repeated disclosures as the child seeks confirmation of the news. Repeated disclosures are also needed as children become more fully aware of the significance of a situation that they have known about for some time, as well as on each occasion that an associated loss arises. A child whose parents have been divorced for a considerable time might only become fully aware of the significance of the situation when one remarries. For some children, their families and professional carers, bad news becomes a repetitive stressor. Children who have a chronic disability or life-threatening condition can be exposed to a series of debilitating episodes during the course of their illness, each one involving new losses and more bad news. Unfortunately adults have a tendency to underestimate the impact of repeated disclosures of bad news, leading to a less sensitive and less helpful approach being used. This is even more likely to happen when repeated losses are associated with a long-standing situation during which the child's perception of what constitutes bad news changes. Thus something that was of little or no concern to the child at an earlier age or different stage of awareness becomes significant and is interpreted as bad news. These are not the only situations when bad news is disclosed insensitively simply because the informing adult does not realise that the news will be interpreted as being bad. Children can be extremely distressed by losses that adults regard as being of less importance. Empathising with children is not easy. Recognising that the essence of bad news is loss, and that a child will probably interpret news as being bad if it involves the loss or the lessening of something or someone valued by that child, can help adults to adopt an empathic view. Continuing to keep in touch with the child's thoughts and feelings is essential throughout the disclosure.

The many situations which involve breaking bad news to children and the frequency with which these occur emphasise the relevance of knowing how bad news can be disclosed in a helpful way. The importance of doing so is underlined by the adverse consequences that can result if it is not and the benefits that can be gained if it is. Although it is difficult to separate the effect of the bad news itself from that of the way in which it is given, it is not unreasonable to suggest that a child's immediate and long-term responses to bad news are influenced by the way in which it is disclosed. Bad news that is broken in an unhelpful way causes additional distress and can delay and prolong the child's coming to terms with the inherent losses. Children can and sometimes do react strongly to bad news. Occasionally these strong reactions result in children harming themselves accidentally or intentionally and even deaths due to carelessness or suicide are not unknown. On the other hand, bad news that is disclosed in a helpful way can lessen the intensity of the child's distress and so reduce any sense of disbelief, sadness, anger, guilt, shame, inadequacy, vulnerability and hopelessness that the child might be feeling. The informing adult is also more likely to be seen as a compassionate and approachable person and become a continuing source of comfort and support. Children are more likely to feel able to talk about their feelings and concerns and respond positively to help offered by others. At a time when the adults involved feel particularly impotent, disclosing bad news in a helpful way gives them a sense of doing something useful. This is extremely important for professional carers repeatedly involved in disclosing bad news and who are therefore especially vulnerable to emotional burnout.

Whether or not to Tell

The decision as to whether or not to tell a child is rarely simple and the decision-making process always difficult. Two opposing views have emerged and given rise to different approaches. The 'protective approach' seeks to shield children from knowing bad news, whereas supporters of the 'open approach' recommend that children should be told.

Arriving at a decision is especially difficult because of the many influential factors and the complexity of the issues involved. These decisions are not based solely on ideology or ethics – issues of emotional comfort are also involved (Chesler *et al.*, 1986). Nor are they based solely on the needs of the child but have to take into account those of others involved. Bluebond-Langner captures the complexity of the situation for those involved with dying children: 'The needs of the children, the parents and staff must all be taken into account; for one dies as a member of society, linked to other individuals. Often these individuals' needs are conflicting' (Bluebond-Langner, 1978, p. 235). Deciding whether or not to tell is made even more difficult when the bad news is associated with stigma or when it includes uncertainties. Disclosing bad news does not have to be an 'all or nothing' situation. Understanding this can influence the decision as to whether or not to tell as well as raising the question of exactly what to disclose. Being selective about what is told and talked about is not without its difficulties, but to be so does not compromise honesty. Honesty does not mean the same as complete openness. There may be aspects of the bad news that all or some of those involved do not wish to talk about. Being honest means acknowledging this.

Much of the debate about whether or not children should be told bad news has taken place in the health-care arena; however, the principles underpinning these arguments can also help to inform the decision-making process when the bad news is about matters that are predominantly social or domestic. In view of the uniqueness of each situation it would be unwise to be dogmatic about whether or not a child should be told, but there are some compelling arguments in favour of the open approach.

Children do become aware of bad news or that something is amiss even when they are not openly told and despite attempts to conceal the news (Waechter, 1971; Bluebond-Langner, 1978; Kendrick *et al.*, 1986; Bearison, 1991). Information acquired in such a haphazard manner is usually distorted and incomplete, increasing the likelihood of the child feeling confused, frightened and lonely. Although disclosing bad news inevitably causes distress, children are likely to experience less distress when given clear and honest information with which to make some sense of what is happening and when they are allowed to share their thoughts and feelings with a trusted adult (Jewett, 1994). The argument that children, especially young ones, do not need to be told because they do not have the capacity to comprehend concepts and abstract notions about illness, death and other sources of bad news ignores the influence of personal or vicarious experience on their understanding. Personal or vicarious experience can influence children's comprehension and result in them acquiring an understanding at an earlier age than those who have not had such experience (Bluebond-Langner, 1978; Reilly *et al.*, 1983; Ross-Alaolmolki, 1985; Eiser, 1990). Furthermore, even young children can be helped to acquire a rudimentary understanding of abstract notions if explanations are given in concrete terms and related to their experience (Jewett, 1994). When children are openly told of bad news they can become actively involved and so benefit from helping themselves and offering help to others affected by the news – something which they often wish to do (Nitschke *et al.*, 1982; Pearson, 1983; Whittham, 1993). The few studies that have been undertaken to determine the effect of being told of bad news on children's short and long-term adjustment suggest that disclosure is beneficial (Slavin *et al.*, 1982; Rosenheim and Reicher, 1985). In addition, it can be argued that children have a right to know about any situation that affects them (Bok, 1978), however, this might conflict with the rights of others and the emotional comfort of all.

Generally speaking the decision should rest with the child's parents or legal guardians. Children who intimate that they want to know what is happening, and even those who make an explicit request to be told, are still dependent on the decision of others as to whether or not they are told. However, once the bad news has been broken, children can and should be given the opportunity of being actively involved in deciding what else they are told and the manner in which they are told. Proponents of the view that children should be told only when they ask, or appear to want to know, rely too heavily on children being able to express themselves and depend too much on their own ability to recognise covert expressions. Furthermore, these children are subjected to isolation, confusion and anxiety until such a time as they feel able to express themselves or their disguised fears and concerns are recognised, which for some may be never.

Professional carers are ideally placed to create a supportive and non-judgemental environment in which to provide information and help those concerned work through the dilemma and arrive at an informed decision. Unfortunately little is known about how families make these decisions, but whatever their cultural origins and persisting influences each family will have a unique set of interactions and conventions with which the professional carer needs to become familiar.

Who Should Tell and Who Else Should be Told

Children are usually helped most when told by the adult to whom they feel closest and with whom they will have a continuing relationship based on a history of trust. This person is usually, but not always, a parent. Because this person is often also upset by the bad news, it is usually helpful and sometimes necessary to have a professional carer involved at the time of disclosure. The professional carer can provide emotional support and information and, if required, can be the one who tells the child. Ideally any professional carer involved in disclosing bad news should:

- have a good relationship with the child and others involved;
- be skilful at disclosing bad news to children and their significant others, and responding to their reactions;

- be sufficiently knowledgeable about the child's condition, the people involved and the circumstances of the specific situation in order to answer questions that might be asked;
- be available to provide support immediately following the disclosure and over a longer period;
- feel able to deal with the specific situation.

The unlikelihood of these criteria being fulfilled by a single person suggests that more than one professional carer should be involved; however, care should be taken not to make the child feel intimidated.

Professional carers are faced with a particularly difficult dilemma when children present them with questions or concerns which should be answered by the parent or only after the parent has been consulted. This situation is especially likely to happen where mutual pretence exists between parent and child. The following suggestion offers professional carers a helpful way of responding to such situations.

Having expressed a concern, the child can be encouraged to share thoughts and feelings by using open questions such as:

'How does that make you feel?'
'What makes you think that?'

This initial response shows children that they are being taken seriously and gives them permission to feel as they feel and think what they think. It also projects the adult as a person who can be approached and enables this person to get a better understanding of the situation as the child sees it. Given an opportunity to talk about their feelings, children are also likely to show them and need to be comforted before proceeding. Once the child's thoughts and feelings have been expressed an empathic response gives further reassurance that this is acceptable and reaffirms the adult's approachability, for example:

'This must be a big worry for you and so I'm pleased you've told me about what's happening and how you feel about it'.

This can be followed by an honest remark about how difficult it is to know what to say but which also contains a suggestion for doing something and an assurance of continuing support:

'It's really difficult for me to know what to say. I think it would help if Mum and Dad know about what you're thinking and just how you feel. We could talk to them together or I could see them on my own. What do you think?'

Children who do not want their parents to be involved are usually trying to protect them from being upset; sometimes children are trying to protect themselves from what they think will be their parents' response. These possibilities can be sensitively explored with the child and where possible reassurance given. The child can be also told that parents know most things about their children and might want to talk about it. One helpful way of responding to a child's continuing reluctance to involve the parents is to talk with the child about those aspects of the parents' behaviour that suggest they already know. Raising a child's awareness of what the parents know often removes the need for pretence and paves the way for open communication. The same approach can also be used with parents when it is they who do not want their child to be told despite evidence that the child already knows. However, neither children nor parents should be pressured into breaking pretence. Despite the problems associated with pretence, neither one-sided pretence, whether on the part of the child or parent, nor mutual pretence, should be automatically challenged – without it they might not be able to relate to each other. Open communication about bad news should be encouraged but not at the expense of child–parent relationships.

In view of the intimacy of family relationships and the numerous other interactions a child is likely to have it is usually helpful and sometimes necessary to inform others. Exactly who is informed will depend on the particular situation; however, it is usually advisable to inform other members of the family, the staff of the child's school and the leaders of clubs to which the child belongs. This helps to promote an understanding response to the child's behaviour and academic performance and increases the support that is available, as well as reducing tension and other adverse effects of collusion. Inevitably some people will be informed before others, but delays increase collusion, even if only temporarily, and therefore are best avoided. In many situations the other children in the family will be told also, but there is a tendency to exclude siblings when it is their brother or sister who is the subject of the bad news. These siblings then become vulnerable to the adverse effects of collusion and are particularly likely to feel resentful of a brother or sister who is receiving special attention and for no apparent reason. When appropriate, children should be involved in making decisions about telling others, especially when the news is about themselves. When other people have already been informed, children should be told who these people are and what they have been told. When there is a stigma associated with the source of the bad news, care needs to be taken about who is told. Children and their families 'must deal with a social environment that contains panic, fear, misinformation and discrimination' (Schaefer and Lyons, 1993, p. 135). This reality is typified by situations when the bad news is about a diagnosis of AIDS. The reasons for being careful and selective about which people are told and what they are told should be explained to the child, for example:

> Daddy has a disease in his blood. It's a new disease and people don't have a good feeling about it. It makes them afraid (Schaefer, 1993, p. 135).

When and Where to Tell

The ideal circumstances for when and where to break bad news are rarely achievable but the following suggestions should be kept in mind and applied whenever possible.

Sooner rather than later. Whether the bad news is about an event that has already occurred or something that is going to happen, children are helped more by being told sooner rather than later. Even when there are uncertainties about what has happened or is about to happen, delaying disclosure is likely to create more anxiety and distress for all concerned. The study by Slavin *et al.* (1982) into the long-term psychological adjustment of survivors of childhood malignancy found that children who had early knowledge of their diagnosis were better adjusted that those who were told later. The prompt disclosure of accurate information about a death helps children to grieve (Bowlby, 1980) and it is not unreasonable to suggest that this is also true of other losses.

When all can be present. Disclosures should take place when all those who need to be involved can be together.

Full attention. A time should be chosen when those involved are able to give their full attention to what is being said and not distracted by being too tired, too ill, or too distressed. The place chosen should be comfortable, quiet, private and free from interruptions.

Among familiar surroundings. The child should be among familiar surroundings, preferably at home, and with comforting possessions at hand.

Where reactions and responses will not be inhibited. The place where bad news is disclosed should not inhibit the child from showing emotions or asking questions, nor make it difficult for the informing adult to provide comfort.

Stay together afterwards. Bad news should be disclosed at a time when those involved are able to stay with each other, at least during the period immediately after the news is broken.

Whenever and wherever bad news is broken it is more likely to be disclosed in a helpful way when it is planned and prepared.

Preparing to Tell

Both proactive and reactive disclosures can be anticipated and therefore planned and prepared. Reactive disclosures are less predictable but can still be anticipated, even if the precise moment of disclosure cannot be predicted. Therefore a response, even if it is to defer giving an answer, can be planned and prepared. Professional carers have an obligation to prepare themselves and a responsibility to offer such help to parents and others. All those involved should work together to plan the most helpful approach to the particular situation. Preparing to disclose bad news involves introspection, empathising, and planning and rehearsing.

Introspection. The adults involved might have strong feelings about the bad news and being involved in the disclosure. Such feelings can interfere and dominate, preventing the disclosure from being as helpful as it might otherwise be. This is more likely to happen when the adults involved are unprepared for how they might feel and how they might behave during the disclosure. Thinking about the following questions and talking them over with a trusted other can help those involved manage their feelings and behave in a more helpful way.

- Do I feel anxious about what has happened?
- Do I feel guilty about what has happened?
- Do I feel vulnerable?
- Do I think I will be blamed for the bad news?
- Do I blame someone for the bad news and if so, who?
- Do I feel relieved about what has happened?
- Do I have expectations about how the child should react?
- Are there any reactions that I find particularly difficult to handle?

- Do I have strong feelings about the child and what are these?
- Do I think that someone else should be doing this?

    Empathising. This involves anticipating what the child is likely to feel and think and how the child might react to the news.

    Planning and rehearsing. Mentally rehearsing and even role-playing an imminent proactive disclosure or an anticipated reactive one can lead to a more helpful disclosure being made.

The course of a disclosure can never be predicted with complete accuracy. The adults involved should always respond to the needs of the child rather than try to adhere to a predetermined plan which becomes no longer appropriate. However, having a number of possible techniques and approaches in mind will increase the likelihood of being able to select the most helpful way of dealing with a particular situation as it develops.

What to Say and How to Say it

Bad news should be gradually and progressively introduced through a series of gentle steps, each one revealing a little more of the news and what it means for the child. In this way the child is gradually prepared by a series of warning shots and the pace of disclosure is slowed so that there is less likelihood of the child being suddenly and completely overwhelmed by emotional shock. Throughout the disclosure emotional support can be given by verbal and non-verbal communications that demonstrate attentiveness and warmth, thereby conveying genuine concern and affirming the child's worth. Those involved should be physically close, preferably sitting beside each other. Younger children can be sat on the adult's lap and even older ones usually appreciate a cuddle. Maintaining eye contact during the disclosure is difficult but helps to reinforce the adult's emotional presence and availability as well as conveying warmth and concern. The child should be spoken to quietly, using a soft tone of voice.

What a child is told should be guided from start to finish by the child's needs and wishes. However, what is disclosed cannot be left entirely to the child. Breaking bad news is an asymmetric process in that it invariably involves imparting information of which the recipient is as yet unaware or unsure (Buckman, 1992). In addition to this unknown information there are likely to be needs and wishes of which the child is unaware or unable to articulate. This calls for some reasonable assumptions to be made by those adults who are involved. Each child will have particular concerns but these are likely to include:

- What has happened?
- What is going to happen?
- Is this true?
- Will I be looked after?
- Is there any hope?
- Am I to blame?
- Can this be put right or made better?
- Am I responsible for putting this right or making things better?
- How can I help?
- Can I trust people?
- Can I trust my own observations and judgements?
- Are my feelings appropriate and is it all right to show these?

Even reasonable assumptions can be misleading and care needs to be taken to ensure that the disclosure remains child-led wherever possible as well as being child-focused throughout. This can be achieved by combining information giving with the process of aligning.

Aligning involves finding out what the child already knows or suspects and remaining receptive and responsive to the child's needs and wishes throughout the disclosure. In this way the child can influence what is disclosed and thereby reduce the chance of the disclosure being dominated by the adult's perception of the child's needs and wishes. Aligning can be alternated with giving information in such a way as to provide a protocol for what to say. This protocol can be used for any bad news and whatever the child's degree of awareness; it can be used for both proactive and reactive disclosures.

Step One. Aligning: finding out what the child already knows or suspects

When there is reason to think that the child is already aware of the bad news or that something is amiss, one way of broaching the subject is to acknowledge openly something that the child has said, or done, or seen, and invite the child to talk about it:

> 'Lately I've noticed you've been asking a lot of questions about your visits to the hospital. That's o.k., but I was wondering if there's a special reason . . .'

'You know Tommy's been falling over a lot lately. Have you ever wondered why . . .'

Aligning is also necessary at the beginning of a reactive disclosure initiated by a child. The informing adult should respond to the child's question or comment by acknowledging what the child has said and that it is important, followed by an open question which encourages the child to say more.

In situations when the news is unexpected and the child knows nothing of what is about to be said, the disclosure can begin at the next step.

Step Two. Informing: telling the child about the bad news

Children should be given factual information about:

- what has happened;
- what is happening;
- what is going to happen;
- what this is likely to mean for them;
- what is being done to help.

This is necessary in order for them to make some sense of the situation and to begin to deal with the bad news. In the absence of clear and reliable information a child is hard pressed to work out what is happening and is left confused, anxious and vulnerable to fantasies that can be more distressing than the reality (Jewett, 1994).

Information can be given sensitively by using a narrative approach. This involves giving a brief and simple, step by step, chronological account of what has happened and what is likely to happen next. Organising thoughts into a temporal sequence is a natural format for talking about experiences (Bearison, 1991) and is therefore easier to use than other organising principles. Such an account should begin with an event of which the child has personal experience. Referring to what a child knows from what the child has seen, heard, or felt, makes the news more credible and the informing adult more trustworthy:

'You know you saw Dad talking to those two policemen . . .'
'You know you've heard Mummy and Daddy shouting at each other lately . . .'
'You know you've been feeling ill a lot lately and the doctor did some tests . . .'

Knowing what is about to happen enables children to prepare themselves by mentally rehearsing these events and how they might feel; anticipatory grieving about future losses can take place. Giving children reliable information about what is going to happen can also help to restore their confidence in the predictability of events and the trustworthiness of people. However, difficulties arise when future events are uncertain or when the situation will gradually worsen over a long period – both of which can be characteristic of chronic illness and disability. These sort of situations present those involved with the dilemma of how much of the future should be revealed at any one time. It is probably of little value to disclose bad news about likely future events which are too remote from the child's current experience for the child to be able to make the necessary connection. Children are more likely to believe bad news when at least some of it is substantiated by their own experience. Bluebond-Langner's observations of terminally ill children reveal that children's personal and vicarious experience is critical to their stage of awareness: 'the disease experience enables them to assimilate . . . information by relating what they saw and heard to their own experience . . .' (Bluebond-Langner, 1978, p. 168). Therefore, when disclosing bad news about events beyond those that are imminent, it is probably best to be guided by what children appear to want to know as a result of what they say or intimate. This child-led as well as child-focused approach to the disclosure of bad news about future events does, however, require parents and professional carers to sustain an open climate of communication and remain receptive and responsive to the child's overt and covert expressions.

As well as being given factual information, children should be given clear explanations in keeping with their vocabulary and cognitive ability. These should also take account of the fact that bad news often includes terms and concepts of which even older children are not familiar. Bad news about medical or legal matters will include professional terms that need careful explanation. Age provides a rough guide to cognitive ability, but the individuality of each child must be taken into account, together with the child's previous experience and current level of stress. Eiser (1990) suggests that a child's beliefs about illness may reflect personal experience as much as any structural change in the ability to understand. Stress usually impairs understanding and may be sufficiently strong to cause a child to regress to behaviours, beliefs and cognitive abilities more in keeping with an earlier stage of development. When communicating with young children it is particularly important to supplement verbal information with non-verbal cues and so create a non-verbal context which helps them understand what is being said (Hyland and Donaldson, 1989). Any indication that the child has not heard or understood should be looked for and explanations repeated or rephrased. In certain circumstances, especially when the child's co-operation is paramount, a more thorough appraisal of the child's understanding is required.

Step Three. Aligning: finding out what else the child wants to know

Children should be asked if there is anything else that they want to know and given an opportunity to talk about their thoughts and feelings. The child's agenda can be safeguarded here and through-out the disclosure by pausing to give the child time to think and speak, by using open questions and by checking exactly what the child means. Buckman (1988) reinforces this last point with the story of a six-year-old girl with leukaemia who asked her mother, 'When will I feel better?'. The mother became very distressed be-cause she thought her daughter was asking about the long-term future when in fact her question referred to the side effects of the chemotherapy she was receiving.

Step Four. Informing: meeting the child's needs and wishes

Information and explanations should be given in response to the needs and wishes expressed or intimated by the child during the previous step. Even if not expressed, the following concerns should always be addressed here or at an earlier point in the disclosure if that becomes necessary or appears to be more appropriate. Each should be addressed with honesty and consistency.

Fear of being abandoned

Even when bad news does not involve separation, because it always involves some sort of loss it can reconnect the child with the early fear of losing someone with whom a strong attachment has been formed – the fear of being abandoned. The associated anxiety can be over-whelming and all children are left feeling vulnerable. The presence of a trusted adult is in itself reassuring and can be reinforced by get-ting physically close to the child. Touch is extremely comforting but should never become a substitute for actually telling children that they will not be left to cope on their own.

When the bad news does involve separation a child's sense of abandonment can be heightened by being told that the absent person is happy or even happier. It is particularly tempting to give this reassurance when someone has died. Although motivated by a desire to reduce emotional pain, this can have the opposite effect and children may feel anger toward someone who appears not to want to be with them (Buckman, 1988). Therefore young children who have not appreciated that death is irreversible can be particularly distressed. However, such feelings are not confined to separations brought about by death and can be experienced by children at any age. Reassurance can still be given without exaggerating the actual or imagined happiness of the absent person.

Self-blame, guilt and shame

Children have a propensity to blame themselves for bad news. Self-blame is usually inappropriate and the result of the magical thinking associated with young children but to which older children can and do regress during times of stress. Just as magical thinking encourages children to blame themselves, so can their sense of immanent justice cause them to feel shame. Feelings of shame can also be occasioned by the stigma associated with some medical, domestic and social situations. Thoughts and feelings of self-blame and shame need to be addressed at the time the bad news is disclosed. Children should be clearly told that neither they nor anyone else is responsible for causing the bad news nor preventing it from happening. Care should be taken to ensure that children do not receive other messages that conflict with these reassurances. Children might be told that a parent's illness or a marital breakdown was not due to anything done by them but overhear remarks that suggest the opposite: 'Of course David was a very demanding child and that couldn't have helped'. Children should also be told that it is not their responsibility to correct the bad news nor to make things better. These reassurances need to be given even when children do not express such thoughts, and usually they do not. It is likely that these thoughts and feelings will occur at sometime. The possibility of creating problems where there are none is minimal compared to the distress caused by self-blame and shame.

Unfortunately, there can be situations when the child or another person is responsible for causing or contributing to the bad news. Dismissing or denying the child's contribution or that of another person is not helpful, however well-meaning, and serves only to foster a climate of closed communication and distrust in which the child is left to deal with these feelings by himself or herself. Instead, the child needs to be helped to put things into perspective. Although this might require long-term professional help, children can and should be helped at the time the bad news is disclosed. The devastating feelings of shame and real culpability cannot be removed but can be offset by reality-testing. Most behaviour can be explained, if not excused, by a lack of knowledge, or how a person felt at the time, or the prevailing circumstances. Conversations which get children to think about these ameliorating factors can help them put things into a perspective with which it is easier to cope.

Helplessness

Bad news can create an overwhelming sense of helplessness. This can be offset at the time of disclosure by reassuring children that they will continue to be informed of what is happening and consulted about decisions when this is appropriate. In circumstances where self-care is an important and perhaps essential part of treatment there are pragmatic as well as ethical reasons for involving the child. Children are capable of making rational decisions either on their own or in conjunction with their family. Nitschke *et al.*, (1982) describe how children with end-stage cancer, some only six years old, are capable of making decisions about their treatment and are willing to do so. Being involved also allows children to participate in activities that help them cope. The emotional and intellectual complexity of adolescence, together with the challenge of accomplishing developmental tasks, means that adolescents are in particular need of being involved in order for them to have the opportunity of experiencing control, autonomy and a sense of belonging (Pazola and Gerberg, 1990). Palmer (1994) highlights the importance of involving adolescent oncology patients and discusses ways of providing them with information. Even when the bad news is about themselves, children are usually concerned about how others are affected and want to help them as much as they can. Children can be helped to find something to do which is both meaningful to them and within their capabilities. Involving children is not without its difficulties and they should be guarded against expecting too much of themselves. Well-intentioned remarks such as: 'You've got to get better for your Mum's sake' and 'While Dad's in hospital you'll have to look after the family' can place an unfair and heavy burden on a child.

Hope is a protective response to bad news – a way of diminishing the intensity of despair and enabling a child to accept gradually the full significance of the bad news. Even children who are dying, and experiencing what would appear to be the most hopeless of situations, have hope: 'There is always some hope, even if not for cure, then for some last wish or achievement to be fulfilled, or for a comfortable last phase, for a death that is peaceful' (Judd, 1993, p. 196). As with a sense of helplessness, the feeling of hopelessness can be offset at the time the bad news is disclosed and realistic hopes nurtured from the outset by:

- giving children accurate and honest information;
- telling them what will be done to help;
- letting them know what they can do to help;
- openly talking about hopes as well as disappointments.

Telling children about others who have coped well in a similar situation can be helpful but can also increase stress by making them think that they must do the same. The temptation to be overly optimistic, or emphasise the better aspects of the situation should be avoided. Children usually regard these as attempts to dismiss the significance of their feelings. Pointing out that some children are in a worse situation has a similar effect. Responding to hopes, even unrealistic ones, with abrupt reminders or revelations of the truth is always insensitive and usually ineffective. Children should neither be given false assurance nor have their remarks casually dismissed or ignored. Children should not be pressured into hoping but nor should they be denied an opportunity to diminish their despair.

Honesty and consistency

Giving information that is honest and consistent helps a child to accept the reality of the bad news and trust those involved. Accepting the reality of a loss is the first task of grieving without which the remaining tasks cannot be undertaken and the grief remains unresolved (Worden, 1991). Without first accepting the reality of the bad news a child will not be able to begin the process of coming to terms with the inherent losses.

Honesty can be achieved without exposing a child to brutal or graphic detail. Terms that are less emotive and upsetting should be chosen, bearing in mind that euphemisms, ambiguities and subtleties only confuse and should be avoided. If the bad news contains uncertainties, these should be acknowledged. False reassurances are usually recognised as such, either at the time or later, and make it difficult for the child to trust those involved. Promises should be given cautiously. Broken promises challenge children's capacity for trust and their sense of reliability, both of which will already have been diminished by the bad news. Nor should an adult pretend to believe in something. Children usually recognise such dissonance which then becomes another source of distress and reason for doubting the trustworthiness of that person. Commitments are inevitably made when talking about the future and these need to be honoured. Any unforeseen circumstances that make it impossible for promises to be kept must be carefully and honestly explained. Children often ask a person the same question time and time again and repeatedly ask others the same question. This is one way in which children seek confirmation of what they have been told and are thus helped to accept the reality of the bad news. This can only be achieved if the information they are given is consistent; good communication and teamwork are therefore crucial.

Maintaining an honest and consistent response is very difficult in the face of a child's repeated demand for promises that the bad news can be put right, but it is possible to give an honest response in a sensitive and helpful way. Buckman gives an example of how this could be done in response to the question, 'When am I going to get better?' He suggests:

> "If we could make you better, we would."

> Which is truthful, and may lead the child to ask:

> "Why can't you make me better?"

> This allows you to say:

> "Sometimes there are things that nobody can fix, no matter how much they would like to" (Buckman, 1988, p. 201).

When an adult feels unable to reply honestly to a child's searching question, falsehoods and glib phrases such as, 'I'll tell you one day' or 'You're too young to understand' should be avoided. More helpful responses can be made:

> 'I can see you're very worried about this and I'm sorry you're upset. It is important but I find it too difficult to talk about right now' or
> 'I can see you're very worried about this and I'm sorry you're upset. It is important but I don't know what the answer is.'

In such circumstances it is usually advisable to seek help and suggesting this provides reassurance that neither the child nor the problem is being dismissed: 'I think we need to talk about this with your social worker'.

One of the questions most dreaded by adults is when the child asks, 'Am I going to die?'. Children do not usually ask this or similar questions in such a direct way unless they have already intuited the truth and are ready to hear it (Pearson, 1983).

Children who are given honest and consistent information, especially when verified by their own observations and experiences, are better placed to: accept the reality of the bad news and begin grieving; test the appropriateness of any guilt or shame they feel; and are less likely to experience distressing fantasies. Not least, the bond of trust between the child and others is maintained and remains a source of support. There is little, if anything, to be gained by telling a falsehood, but much to be gained by telling the truth in a sensitive and helpful way.

How to Respond

Children are likely to react at any time during the disclosure and a comforting response should not be deferred. For convenience, their possible reactions are considered separately.

A child's experience with loss is greatly influenced by the extent to which adults allow the child to experience the accompanying strong emotions (Jewett, 1994). When bad news is broken, important messages about the appropriateness of the child's reaction are inevitably and often unwittingly sent. Thus positive or negative ground rules are established for the process of coming to terms with the inherent losses. Four important messages need to be conveyed to the child:

- there are no right or wrong feelings and even those about which the child might feel ashamed are not uncommon nor unreasonable;
- it is helpful to express feelings;
- there are no right or wrong ways to express feelings (although children need to be protected from harming themselves or others);
- the child will be supported and helped to work through feelings.

These messages should not merely be implied – they must be made explicit.

Although it is difficult to predict how a child will react to bad news, it is helpful to know of the ways in which the child might react. This will lessen the surprise and thereby increase the likelihood of making a helpful response. Children may feel a variety of emotions in response to bad news: numbness, anxiety, fear, disbelief, denial, anger, guilt, shame, sadness, loneliness and despair. The emotions they feel might not be displayed for some time. Some reactions to bad news can appear strange and inappropriate, making it difficult for adults to respond helpfully. Children can sometimes appear to dismiss the importance of the bad news or their relationship with the person to whom it refers. Some children display relief at being told. For some the bad news itself brings a sense of genuine relief which is concealed initially, only to manifest itself later in the form of guilt feelings. These sort of reactions usually can be explained in terms of self-protection or the child's inability to comprehend the significance of the news. It is not uncommon for a child to feel several different and even conflicting emotions simultaneously. Some indication as to how a particular child might react can be gained by considering:

- how the child has reacted to previous losses and stressful events;
- the child's personality;
- the child's ability to understand the significance of the bad news;
- the physical surroundings;
- the child's relationship with those who are to be present;
- the child's ethnic background;
- the culture and dynamics of the child's particular family;
- the way in which the bad news is to be given.

Specific reactions require particular responses but whatever the child's reaction, applying the following principles can help.

Stay with the child. The presence of a trusted adult is in itself reassuring, and physical contact is comforting at any age, although some older children might prefer to be left on their own and go for a walk or seek solitude in their room.

Accept their thoughts and feelings. Children need to work through their own feelings, whatever these are, in an uninhibited way, provided this does not compromise the safety of themselves or others.

Empathise. Children need to know that their feelings are recognised without being antagonised by statements that imply knowledge of exactly what they are feeling. Empathic statements such as 'I can see you are upset; this must be so very hard for you' can help to do this.

Share feelings. The mutual expression of thoughts and feelings helps to create an open and honest environment in which children can ask questions, talk about their anxieties and express their thoughts and feelings. Sharing thoughts and feelings helps to prevent a child from feeling isolated and gives the child an opportunity to offer as well as receive comfort. However, children should not be allowed to feel responsible for comforting distressed adults. Nor should they be allowed to feel confused or guilty about having thoughts and feelings that are different from those of others.

Encourage talking. All the previous principles of responding will help children to talk about their thoughts and feelings. On occasions, however, a little more help might be needed. This is not an appropriate time to expose children to any in-depth probing, but help can be given by empathically acknowledging the difficulty and asking them if they would like to talk about their feelings: 'Lots of people find it difficult to talk about their feelings, but it can help. Would you like to tell me about yours?'. If the response is negative: 'That's o.k., we can always talk later if you want to'. And if the response is affirmative: 'What sort of things are you feeling?'

Additional comforts. These can always be provided to meet the particular needs and wishes of the individual child.

Conclusion

Bad news always involves the loss or lessening of something or someone valued by the child. Despite the inevitable distress caused by breaking bad news there are compelling reasons for telling children. These include the views of children themselves and are supported by evidence that children become aware of bad news even when they are not told and despite attempts to conceal the news. Breaking bad news in an honest and sensitive way helps children accept the reality of the loss, without which they cannot begin to grieve. In the absence of an open, honest, non-judgemental and supportive environment children are left feeling confused, anxious and lonely. Open communication about bad news should be encouraged but not at the expense of the child–parent relationship. Professional carers are ideally placed to help all concerned deal with the dilemmas and difficulties of breaking bad news.

This chapter has focused on the technique of breaking bad news.

to children and suggested one which can be used by professional carers and shared with parents and others. A set of principles has been proposed which takes into account the needs and individuality of all involved, adults as well as children, together with the circumstances of the particular situation. These principles have been incorporated in and clustered around a protocol for breaking bad news to children. This protocol is child-focused throughout and remains sufficiently flexible to be child- led wherever possible.

References

Bearison, D. (1991) *"They Never Want to Tell You". Children Talk About Cancer*. Cambridge, Massachusetts: Harvard University Press.

Bluebond-Langner, M. (1978) *The Private Worlds of Dying Children*. Princeton: Princeton University Press.

Bok, S. (1978) *Lying: Moral Choice in Public and Private Life*. Hassocks: Harvester Press.

Bowlby, J. (1980) *Attachment and Loss, Volume 3: Loss: Sadness and Depression*. London: The Hogarth Press.

Buckman, R. (1988) *"I Don't Know What to Say . . .". How to Help and Support Someone Who is Dying*. London: Papermac.

Buckman, R. (1992) *How to Break Bad News. A Guide for Health-Care Professionals*. London: Papermac.

Chesler, M.A., Paris, J. and Barbarin, O.A. (1986) "Telling" the child with cancer: parental choices to share information with ill children. *Journal of Pediatric Psychology*, **11**: 497.

Eiser, C. (1990) *Chronic Childhood Disease. An Introduction to Psychological Theory and Research*. Cambridge: Cambridge University Press.

Hyland, M.E. and Donaldson, M.L. (1989) *Psychological Care in Nursing Practice*. London: Scutari Press.

Jewett, C. (1994) *Helping Children Cope with Separation and Loss*. London: Batsford.

Judd, D. (1993) Communicating with dying children. In D. Dickenson, M. Johnson (Eds), *Death, Dying and Bereavement*. London: Open University Press and Sage Publications.

Kendrick, C., Culling, J., Oakhill, T. and Mott, M. (1986) Children's understanding of their illness and its treatment within a paediatric oncology unit. *Association for Child Psychology and Psychiatry Newsletter*, **8**: 16.

Nitschke, R., Humphrey, G.B., Sexauer, C.L., Catron, B., Wunder, S. and Jay, S. (1982) Therapeutic choices made by patients with end stage cancer. *Journal of Pediatrics*, **101**: 471.

Palmer, S. (1994) Providing information to adolescent oncology patients. *Oncology Nursing*, **6**: 18.

Pazola, K.J. and Gerberg, A.K. (1990) Privileged communication – Talking with a dying adolescent. *American Journal of Maternal Child Nursing*, **15**: 16.

Pearson, J.M. (1983) Terminally ill children. How to discuss death with patients and their families. *Consultant*, **23**: 85.

Reilly, T.P., Hasazi, J.E. and Bond, L.A. (1983) Children's conceptions of death and personal mortality. *Journal of Pediatric Psychology*, **8**: 21.

Rosenheim, E. and Reicher, R. (1985) Informing children about a parent's terminal illness. *Journal of Child Psychology and Psychiatry*, **26**: 995.

Ross-Alaolmolki, K. (1985) Supportive care for families of dying children. *Nursing Clinics of North America*, **20**: 457.

Schaefer, D. and Lyons, C. (1993) *How Do We Tell the Children?* New York: Newmarket Press.

Slavin, L.A., O'Malley, J.E., Koocher, G.P. and Foster, D.J. (1982) Communication of the cancer diagnosis to pediatric patients: impact on long-term adjustment. *American Journal of Psychiatry*, **139**: 179.

Waechter, E. (1971) Children's awareness of fatal illness. *American Journal of Nursing*, **71**: 1168.

Whittham, E.H. (1993) Terminal care of the dying child. Psychosocial implications of care. *Cancer*, **71**: 3450.

Worden, J.W. (1991) *Grief Counselling and Grief Therapy. A Handbook for the Mental Health Practitioner*. London: Tavistock Routledge.

4
Expected and Unexpected Loss

Bridget Hallam and Penny Vine

The aim of this chapter is to identify the different types of loss experienced in childhood, to discuss some of the effects of these losses and to highlight how signs of grief in children can be recognised. The role of professionals working with grieving children will be discussed and the importance of working in partnership with carers emphasised. We will identify some of the needs of children in loss situations and offer suggestions for approaches and resources which can be used to help children resolve their grief.

We define expected loss as that which the child is aware of and can prepare for in advance. Unexpected loss may be the result of a sudden, unanticipated event or more often may arise because, as a result of a child's developmental stage, the child is not able to anticipate the event. In the second of these situations, work can still be done by carers and professionals to prepare for the child's grief and to plan helping strategies.

Our aim is to consider all aspects of loss and grief in childhood rather than concentrating simply on bereavement and other major forms of loss. The rationale for this is that, although we recognise the unique nature of an individual child's grief, children experiencing loss show a range of common feelings and behaviours. The general strategies for helping grieving children can therefore be applied in any situation. What will vary is the depth of grief experienced by individual children. This is influenced by many factors and these will be referred to throughout the text.

Necessary or Developmental Loss

From birth, children experience changes involving separation and loss as part of their normal development. The weaning process, learning to care for personal needs and the body changes associated with the onset of puberty are examples of what Lendrum and Syme (1992) describe as necessary changes. While these form an essential part of the progression towards adulthood, for many children they may be the source of some distress. Children need the support of caring adults for whom they have a strong attachment to enable them to resolve their feelings of loss in these situations. Where appropriate comfort is given these losses, though rarely remembered, will be integrated into the childrens' experience and will provide a firm foundation for their ability to cope in the future.

Many developmental losses are unrecognised or discounted as insignificant. Schneider (1984) argues that unless these are resolved a child's, or indeed an adult's ability to complete mourning on future occasions will be impaired. He also suggests that, although the mourning process may in some cases disrupt development by altering an individual's expectations and perceptions of the world, it may also contribute to it by providing an opportunity for growth and resolution of experience.

Children, Loss and Grief

Studies by Bowlby (1971, 1973) clearly showed that infants as young as six months form very strong attachments to primary care givers. They also experience significant grief reactions, even to a brief separation from the object of their attachment. He believes, however, that children are fully capable of resolving losses if they have a reasonably secure relationship with their parents prior to the loss, if they receive prompt and accurate information about the loss, if they are allowed to participate in family grieving and if they have a continuing secure relationship with a caring adult. Already we have begun to identify the needs of a grieving child and an expansion on these will be found later in the chapter.

A child's loss differs from that of an adult in several ways. Developmentally, children are less equipped to cope with loss. Depending upon their age, their experience and cognitive skills are likely to be limited and their ability to make sense of their experience subsequently reduced. They also have less control over their circumstances and environment than adults, so they have to depend on others, firstly to recognise that they are grieving, and then to anticipate and fulfil their needs.

Even if children are able to make sense of and express their needs, these can be overlooked or vetoed by adults. Often carers will themselves be grieving or will feel they wish to protect the child from further hurt and distress. It may be that the loss appears trivial and is therefore minimised, but the loss of a treasured Teddy or a first boyfriend or girlfriend can be of great significance to a child. In cases where loss is not acknowledged, the grief experienced by children is not lessened, but they are denied the process of mourning which enables them to resolve it.

External Loss

Developmental losses associated with change have already been discussed. Its easy to assume that, excluding these experiences, loss in childhood is uncommon. This is not the case. Throughout childhood external events occur which inevitably result in loss and the need for a child to grieve and reconcile their experiences. Going to a childminder, starting school, moving house or schools, serious illness or hospitalisation, the death of a pet and the break-up of friendships are only a few examples of the losses experienced by most children throughout their lives. Even the birth of a sibling can be associated with feelings of loss as the first child wrestles with the awareness that they may have lost their unique position in the family. The common factor in all these is the loss or feared loss of a significant attachment.

The most researched and obvious examples of this are the losses experienced through the death of a loved one and through divorce or family break-up. While children's encounters with death are thankfully relatively uncommon, it is estimated that up to 50 percent of children will experience divorce or family break-up at some time in their pre-adult lives (Wold, 1981). Working in community and school health it is not uncommon to meet children who have been through multiple losses of this kind even in their pre-school years.

Very often the loss of a stable family environment will be accompanied by further losses such as the need to move house or schools, loss of contact with other family members and even the loss of family pets. All children, including those who may not show obvious signs of grief, need the support of caring adults to enable them to validate their feelings and incorporate their losses into their life experience. Where there has been family violence or abuse, the effects on a child will be compounded and may require specialist intervention. This will be discussed in greater detail in later chapters.

Inner Loss

Not all loss is caused by separation. Children can experience a whole range of inner losses such as loss of identity, confidence or self-esteem, which may or may not be linked to external events. Take, for example, the case of Jamie, who at seven couldn't remember which of three surnames he was using that particular week; or Donna who after seven burglaries at her home in six months refused to sleep alone or let her mother out of her sight. Luke, at the age of 15 suffered a tremendous loss of self-esteem and expectations when he failed to do as well in his exams as he had hoped. These inner losses are often difficult for a child to articulate, so may manifest as behavioural difficulties or even physical symptoms. It is of vital importance to the children that these losses are recognised and taken seriously.

Special mention should be made of the extra pressures that young people face as they enter adolescence. Adolescence has been described as 'leaving the secret garden of childhood' (Murdock, 1987) and 'a time of life when the only thing you can be sure of is that you won't be sure about anything' (Vine, 1994). During adolescence a young person has to cope with specific stresses relating to body image, self-concept, relationships, peer pressure, sexual identity and parental expectations. It is not surprising that these factors, combined with increased independence and the gradual withdrawal from parental influence, can result in a child experiencing overwhelming feelings of loss and insecurity. Although adolescents experience these very strong feelings, they fear losing control over their emotions and often mask their reactions through their behaviour using increased sexual activity, risk taking activities or conflict with their environment as outlets for their grief (Dyregrov, 1991).

Expected and Unexpected Loss

In many cases a loss can be anticipated. Depending on their developmental stage, children can be prepared and take part in preparing themselves for the future. By allowing children to share in events, whether it be the terminal illness of a relative, a divorce or simply moving house, they have time to begin to work through the grief process and to know that those around them are aware of their feelings and recognise them as important. Preparing children for a loss gives them the opportunity to say goodbye and to develop coping strategies for the time when that loss actually occurs.

Even when the child may be too young to anticipate it, work can be done by the adults around them to try and prepare the ground, so that when the event actually happens it does not have the effect of totally rocking the child's stability. Plans can be made to deal with the practical aspects of a situation so that day-to-day routines and care are maintained as far as possible. Children can be introduced to the concepts of loss by discussion and by the use of books or other resources. Although they may not be able to relate these hypothetical situations to future events in their own lives, when the loss occurs it will at least have some familiarity and the foundations for understanding will have been built. Some examples of situations where these kinds of preparations might be used include the preparation of a young child for starting school, for the birth of a sibling or for the death of a grandparent.

Sudden losses are more difficult for children to cope with. They are often associated with traumatic events that adults themselves find difficult to accept and have difficult in discussing with children. The child has no time for mental preparation and is often plunged suddenly into an insecure world of grieving with little or no explanation. In the case of sudden death, Dyregrov (1991) stresses the importance of distinguishing between after effects caused by the nature of a traumatic death and grief reactions. He highlights the need for children to be given support in working through trauma as well as grief in situations where, for example, they may have witnessed the death or have discovered the body of a parent who has committed suicide. If children are not given this opportunity, he suggests, the grieving process may be slowed or stop altogether.

The Recognition of Grief in Children

Wolfelt (1992) describes some common myths relating to grief:

- a child's grief and mourning is short in duration;
- there is a predictable and orderly stage-like progression to the experiences of grief and mourning;
- the goal in helping bereaved children is to 'get them over' grief and mourning.

He makes the point that children will respond to grief in many different ways and stresses the importance of allowing them to give outward expression to their grief by mourning in a way that is appropriate for them. Just as there is no one way to mourn, there is no fixed formula to describe the grief process and no timetable for its completion.

Although this process is not fixed, certain reactions are common and experienced by most grieving children, if only briefly. Immediate reactions to loss include: shock and disbelief, dismay, protest, apathy or the continuation of usual activities. Children often respond to an initial loss with disbelief. It is as if by denying that something has happened they can keep their grief at a distance. This can be disturbing for carers but should be recognised as a protective mechanism enabling the child to manage loss at their own pace.

The same mechanism is operating where children appear to accept their loss with little reaction. Again, carers may find this response difficult to cope with particularly if they too are grieving. In contrast some children respond to loss with immediate despair and can be inconsolable until the object of their grief reappears or until they are emotionally exhausted (Dyregrov, 1991).

Following these initial reactions, children may show a whole range of grief responses, but again common manifestations include: anxiety, sadness, anger, guilt, shame, disorganization, searching, sleep disturbances and physical symptoms (Wells, 1988). Such reactions to grief are not always clear cut and can be misinterpreted, particularly if the cause of grief has not itself been fully acknowledged by carers. Even in cases where it appears clear that a child has suffered significant loss, the fact that a child's behaviour is the result of grieving can go unrecognised. These reactions to grief will be picked up in more detail as we examine the needs of a grieving child.

The Grief Needs of Children

As we have made clear, each grieving child will experience a unique variety of thoughts, feelings and behaviours. At the same time, just as there are common elements to the grieving process, there is a broad brush stroke of grief needs that children may encounter. The individual child's needs will be dictated by different levels of understanding and ability. The most common needs are:

- for reassurance where this is possible;
- to ask questions – the how, the why, the when – coupled with the need to receive honest answers which should always be factual and age appropriate;
- to have grief recognised and to be taken seriously;
- for emotional support to feel secure enough to express their feelings, which may include both rational and irrational fear, pain, sadness, anger, frustration, disappointment, doubt, guilt, despair, loneliness and insecurity;
- to be allowed to mourn in a way that is appropriate for them;
- to be part of the family loss in the case of a family bereavement;
- to be allowed to cry, regardless of age or sex;
- to share their grief through talking, play or artwork;
- to say goodbye;
- for physical contact;
- for a break in grieving;
- to realise that it's acceptable to begin to enjoy themselves and be happy.

Reassurance

Children who have experienced separation or divorce need the reassurance that they are loved and valued by both parents even though the family structure has changed or is in the process of changing. They need reassurance about the basics of life such as where they will live, when will they see the other parent and if they are not living nearby, how they will maintain contact with that parent. It is also important that they know that the separation was not their fault.

The reassurance needed by children who have experienced the death of someone close to them will be on several levels and may depend on the cause of the death. The grieving child will need assuring that remaining significant adults are safe and will return to them after working or shopping. In the case of death through illnesses such as cancer, they need to know that the disease isn't catching. Children often feel guilty if they have been angry with their parent or sibling prior to their death and need to know that although thought cannot bring back someone they love, it can't kill either.

In all cases of loss, children need the reassurance provided by being in a stable environment. Day-to-day routines should be maintained where possible and attendance at schools or playschools resumed as soon as the child is able to cope with it. Many carers find it difficult to discipline a grieving child yet pushing against the boundaries of acceptable behaviour and finding limits is often a child's way of checking that their world is functioning normally. Far from distressing the child, gentle but firm discipline provided by a caring adult will help them regain a sense of security.

Honest answers

The need for honest answers is linked to the need for reassurance. Death can be explained truthfully and gently. The fact that it's unfair, unkind and makes people very sad can be acknowledged. Honesty is vital for all grieving children. By answering questions honestly you are admitting the child's grief and validating their feelings, whatever the cause.

Recognition of grief

Lendrum and Syme (1992) describe how adults introduce an embarrassed denial of death with young children. In western societies, children are rarely given any information about death, and carers claim that, by withholding this information, they are protecting the child. They will often go to lengths to deflect conversation in an attempt to protect themselves from the child's difficult feelings and questions. In fact by employing these techniques, the adult can deprive the child of their own ways of managing grief and overcoming the effects of loss.

In cases of circumstantial loss other than bereavement, the child's grief is often disregarded. This is done by encouraging the child to focus entirely on the gain in a given situation rather than loss and gain. A common illustration of this is given by well meaning attempts to 'cheer up' children who are to become part of a restructured family with comments such as: 'Aren't you lucky, now you'll have a new daddy, a new brother and two new sisters.'

This insensitive approach denies any loss of intimacy they might fear between themselves and the parent who is to join the new family. It also denies the often deep and genuine feelings of guilt, hurt and loss in relation to their other parent.

Adults must recognise the child's ability to grieve and be prepared to admit this, even when to do so means they will share in that grief themselves, often on top of their own pain.

Sharing grief

Following the death of a loved person or a pet, some children will want to talk about the deceased. This desire to remember in words the person who has died is not to imply that the grieving child will immediately want to talk about mum, dad, grandparent, sibling or friend. Often they will be reticent in an attempt to avoid the pain they are feeling. Another reason they avoid talking about the cause of their grief is a genuine endeavour to shield the adults around them from their pain. This shouldn't be mistaken for the possibility that the child has 'got over it'. Any adult who has experienced the death of a loved family pet will realise how fatuous a comment like 'Well you can soon get another one', or 'it was only a dog' really is.

Children with chronic illness, disability or conditions requiring daily medication need to be allowed and encouraged to talk about their conditions during their spells of grief at their loss of 'problem free health'. Many children who find it difficult to talk about grief and its cause will benefit from artwork. At times it is easier and more comfortable to express your feelings with crayons, felt tips or paints. Young children may also 'play out' their feelings with toys. Children who are stuck in grief may need more specialist help involving structured games led by specialist counsellors and therapists (Davis, 1989).

Saying goodbye

Children need the opportunity to say goodbye, whether it be to school friends as they move to another part of the country, to a parent moving out of the family home or to a relative with a terminal illness. Often adults try to spare children the pain of goodbyes, but they are essential if the child is going to be able to accept their loss. Giving a child time to work through parting enables them to say the things they want to say to loved ones and to ask questions;

particularly to check they are not to blame for the separation. It enables them to plan ways of remembering and to begin grieving. Very often saying goodbye is one of the first steps in a child's beginning to reconcile its grief.

In situations of sudden loss or where the child is developmentally immature, goodbyes can be missed. Children still need the opportunity to say their farewells, and this can require visits to, or communication with, those from whom they have parted. In the case of a death, goodbyes can be said at a funeral or memorial service. Occasionally the goodbye will need to be symbolic and could take the form of a letter or imagined phone call to the absent person. Jewett (1984) advises that actual goodbyes should take place before or as soon as possible after loss occurs. However, she suggests that a symbolic goodbye should only take place at the end of the grieving process as a final act when carers can be sure the child is ready for the parting.

Physical contact

Professionals and carers should be sensitive to the individual grieving child's circumstances and any physical contact should be offered rather than given. The child's acceptance or rejection of the offer should be accepted. The offer need not be verbal – a pair of welcoming arms or an extended hand will convey the message eloquently.

> At a candlelight ceremony during a camp for bereaved children, Sandy, an eight-year-old girl whose father had died when she was five, sat next to Meg, whose father had died just six months previously. The ceremony was one of remembrance. The circle of light was formed by a candle lit by all the children and adults in the circle. Each individual was encouraged to say who the lighted candle represented and one special thing about that person. When it was Sandy's turn, she lit her candle and told everyone that it was for her dad and that she loved and missed him. Then Meg lit her candle and set it on the floor. No sound came, just silence and a little girl with head bowed staring at her candle. Sandy bent forward, looked into Meg's face, raised her eyebrows and slowly stroked Meg's back. Then she hugged her and said 'Meg's candle is for her dad and she loves and misses him too'. That hug comforted Meg and everyone else in the circle as well. (Vine, 1994)

A break in grieving

All children deserve a break in their grieving (Zimmerman, 1994). The ethos underpinning the support camps for bereaved children both here and in the USA is very similar. They make it clear that it is all right to get rid of sad feelings and make room for happy ones. This does not only apply to bereaved children. Any child who has experienced a loss, particularly if as a result of separation, needs this reassurance. Many children feel guilty for starting to enjoy life, particularly if those around them are still sad. They may feel they are betraying those they were grieving for and even feel a need to lapse back into obvious mourning to show they still care. One of the greatest needs of a grieving child is to be helped towards reconciling grief and to be given permission to resume a normal life.

The Role of Carers and Professionals in Supporting Grieving Children

Ideally the most important helper for a grieving child is an active involved parent (Schneider, 1984). In many cases the parent can provide all the help a child needs, but may need support in accomplishing this. The first role of the professional working with grieving children is therefore to act as a sounding board for carers, to give them strength when they feel unable to cope with the challenging behaviour of an angry teenager or distressed toddler, and to provide an opportunity for the carers themselves to ask questions and share their grief. Support may be given by helping carers to plan coping strategies and directing them to suitable resources they could use with the child.

There are cases requiring more direct professional intervention. Parents may be experiencing difficulty in expressing their own grief and may find it hard even to recognise that their child has also experienced a loss. This is very common in situations of marital or family breakdown where parents express surprise that their child is having difficulties at school or has started wetting the bed. Many of these problems continue after the parent has started a new relationship and they find it difficult to understand that the child's reaction to the situation can be so different from their own. Loss resulting from, for example, starting school or difficulties in friendships is very often not recognised as such, and tantrums or other behaviour problems are simply put down to naughtiness. The involved professional needs to talk through the needs of the child and help the carer identify the 'problem' behaviour as a sign of grieving. Not until this has been achieved can plans be developed in conjunction with parents and all involved agencies to provide support for the child. Good and regular communication between professionals is important to ensure the child receives continuity of care.

Some children feel unable to communicate their grief to carers because they wish to spare them distress, because they feel they will be misunderstood or because they feel they may not be given honest answers. This can be a difficult situation for professionals. Every effort should be made to encourage the child to confide in the carers and yet, where at all possible, their confidentiality should be respected. In these circumstances the child needs to feel there is someone who will respect their feelings. This highlights some common elements of practice for professionals working with grieving children and their families.

Common Elements for Practice

Honesty and openness

Those professionals whose work currently includes child protection will already be accustomed to, and hopefully comfortable with, working in an honest and open way with clients. All professionals should be open and honest in their work with children and their families in situations of grief. Honesty in answering questions, however awkward or painful, is vital whether they relate to death, separation, a change in body image or prospects following exam failure. Parents and carers should be encouraged to be equally open and honest. If they find this difficult they can be helped to look at the reasons for their difficulty and hopefully given the support to overcome them. Where the answer to a question is not known, don't be afraid to admit this. Admit your humanity and either find out the answer or, if it is out of your area of expertise, find someone else who can help.

Appropriate explanations

Children do not appreciate being 'talked down to', neither do they benefit from explanations they cannot understand. When this happens they are left frustrated, confused and possibly reluctant to seek further clarification. Developmentally appropriate terms should always be used along with the honest and open approach. At both

Camp Amanda in the USA and Camp Winston in Gloucestershire, there is a 'doctor slot'. Even though these camps are specifically for bereaved children there is a lesson in the use of appropriate explanations to be learned by every professional.

> The children are given the opportunity to ask the doctor questions. This is a group activity and the adult members of the camp attend too. The children ask the most searching questions about life, illness, disability, death, magical thinking, in fact anything that might be puzzling them. The answers come in what the Americans describe as 'ten cent words' or what we might describe as 'child sized words'. That is, in language the children understand. Complex and important questions are dealt with that might otherwise go unanswered and complicate the child's grief. (Vine, 1994)

Creating a 'safe' environment for expression of grief

A 'safe' environment for a grieving child of any age is created as much by the professional involved as by the physical environment. Ideally the area should be quiet, uncluttered, not overlooked by others and comfortable (Jones, 1979). Health professionals rarely have access to such ideal surroundings although there appears to be a welcome increase in quiet, discreet areas being provided in GP surgeries, hospitals and schools.

A child needs to be given time. Five minutes between other appointments is not going to make them feel valued or allow them to express even a fraction of what they are feeling. Like any other supporting situation, the help given must be centred on the needs of the child, and professionals should bring to the environment their counselling skills such as empathy, active listening and reflection.

Cultural and religious differences

Professionals working with grieving children need to be aware of the beliefs about death, the after-life and mourning practices in our multi-ethnic and multi-faith society (Lendrum and Syme, 1992). Attitudes to children and their roles within the family also show wide variation and need to be understood. Obviously a study of comparative religions is not necessary to offer sympathy and support to a grieving child and their family. However, awareness and acceptance of very real differences is essential.

Practical Strategies for Helping Grieving Children

We've already suggested that some children will benefit from the use of imaginative play, artwork or specific games to facilitate the grieving process. These methods may help the child ease into the discussion of difficult feelings, often by first allowing those feelings to be owned by a third party. Specialist books on a whole range of topics from the death of a pet to the understanding that one is adopted can be used in the same way. Questions can be asked about the feelings of the characters in the book rather than those of the specific child. They can also be used to validate the child's own experience and let them know that others have been through similar situations.

A child's need to remember and to be able to talk about the person from whom they are separated can be helped by the use of memory boxes: collections of mementos that have a special significance. These can be used in a wide range of situations and can be planned from the time a loss is anticipated or built retrospectively as a way of giving the child permission to talk about what they feel and what they miss about the person or place being remembered. Parents often start memory boxes for their children when a separation is anticipated and if the child is old enough they can be involved in deciding what will have special memories for them. Scrapbooks are another useful way of encouraging and allowing children to remember. When children are separated permanently from their families they can often suffer a loss of identity and need to know who they are and where they came from. Specialist books are available to give them the information they need in a form that is of value to them.

On a smaller scale but following the same theme, where there is a short- term separation, children often benefit from keeping something significant belonging to the object of their attachment with them. A mother's nightdress or teeshirt can have a very comforting effect on a baby coming to terms with sleeping alone at night, and photographs or tape recordings can provide similar comfort to older children.

As we've suggested, some children, particularly older ones, have the need to talk to someone outside the family. Often this person may be a teacher or school nurse, but sometimes they can, like family, be too close or have too much the ring of authority. If this is so, youth clubs, drop-in advice centres and telephone helplines can provide valuable support for a young person in a non-threatening and non-judgemental way. In cases of bereavement, specialist bereavement groups can be of tremendous help to all children, but particularly those who may be struggling with their grief and finding it difficult to communicate. Such groups are common in the USA and although scarce in this country, their numbers are increasing. Many hospices run special sessions for different age groups of children who have suffered a bereavement and provide the peer support and other care which these children find so valuable (Cohen, 1994).

Education is all important if children are to be helped to grieve effectively. It is needed for children, carers and professionals. Children can begin to understand some of the issues surrounding loss, death and grief by using small examples from their day-to-day lives as the basis for discussion. Even the fate of a woodlouse, trampled as it crosses the pavement, can form the basis for deep debate and give an opportunity to introduce some of the ideas a child will need to reconcile at some time. For older children, the issues may be raised during Personal and Social Education classes at secondary school. It should be remembered though that out of every class of around 30 there may well be a grieving child, and this possibility should be anticipated and planned for.

Parents and carers frequently need education to help them to anticipate and plan for the losses their children may encounter throughout their lives, particularly where those losses might not be immediately obvious. Individual input from health visitors, school nurses, child care nurses and many other professionals can be highly effective in this respect and parenting groups run by them can provide the opportunity for sharing experiences and ideas. The professionals need ongoing training and updating if they are to be able to work effectively with grieving children and their families. It is difficult to be honest and open if your aims are unclear and you lack confidence in your ability and knowledge to provide the support that may be needed.

Conclusion

Experiences of loss frighten most adults, so imagine how they must trouble children. Adults usually approach such problems with some clear philosophy but children have yet to clarify their ideas and it is this understanding that needs to colour all our dealings with grieving children. Distinctions have been made between different kinds of loss in childhood. Fifty percent of children will experience loss through family break-up before adulthood: pets and friends will pass out of an individual's life in the normal course of things, and more abstract events such as the loss of childhood through puberty are inevitable. Although not all loss is expected, where it can be predicted, appropriate preparation can help children through grief and to reconcile loss.

Grief in children may show itself in many ways, including the absence of any obvious reaction to the triggering event – indeed the only reliable indicator of grieving may be that a child has suffered a loss in the first place. It is essential that childhood losses are recognised and acknowledged by families and professionals. In turn, grief produces a range of needs, some of which have been listed. Adults supporting grieving children must anticipate these needs and respond to them in ways appropriate to the child's age and stage of development.

Professionals of all disciplines can play a vital role in ensuring that children experiencing expected or unexpected loss receive the help and support they need. Advice, information and practical assistance can be provided for carers; professionals may step in when carers are unable to provide appropriate support, and they can give grieving adults the additional help they may need in coming to terms with their own grief and that of their children. To be effective, professionals too need to reconcile their own experiences of grief, to have caring support networks and to receive appropriate training for what is a rewarding and at times extremely challenging area of work.

References

Bowlby, J. (1971) *Attachment and Loss. Volume 1: Attachment.* Harmondsworth, Middlesex: Penguin.

Bowlby, J. (1973) *Attachment and Loss. Volume 2: Separation.* Harmondsworth, Middlesex: Penguin.

Cohen, P. (1994) The loss adjusters. *Nursing Times*, **90** (9): 14–15.

Davis, C. (1989) The use of art therapy and group process with grieving children. *Issues in Comprehensive Paediatric Nursing*, **12**: 269–280.

Dyregrov, A. (1991) *Grief in Children – a Handbook for Adults.* London: Jessica Kingsley.

Jewett, C. (1984) *Helping Children Cope with Separation and Loss.* London: Batsford Academic and Educational.

Jones, A. (1979) *Counselling Adolescents in School.* London: Kogan Page.

Lendrum, S. and Syme, G. (1992) *Gift of Tears.* London: Routledge.

Murdock, M. (1987) *Spinning Inward – Using Guided Imagery with*

Children for Learning, Creativity and Relaxation. Boston, Massachusetts: Shambhala Publications.

Schneider, J. (1984) *Stress, Loss and Grief.* Baltimore: University Park Press.

Vine, P. (1994) Personal communication.

Wells, R. (1988) *Helping Children Cope with Grief.* London: Sheldon Press.

Wold, S. (1981) *School Nursing. A Framework for Practice.* London: Mosby.

Wolfelt, A. (1992) Ten common myths about children and grief – Part 1. *Bereavement Magazine*, January 38–40.

Zimmerman, J. (1994) *Amanda the Panda – the Bear with a Heart. A Commitment to Ill and Grieving Children.* Des Moines: Amanda the Panda.

5
Planning an Organisational Response

Elizabeth Capewell

This chapter is about the ways in which organisations such as hospitals, hospices, schools, children's homes and those providing specialist support can prepare for coping on an organisational level when children in their care experience loss and grief, which may or may not be shared by staff. It assumes that the organisation has some responsibility for dealing with the emotional as well as the physical and practical implications of the loss on children and staff. It also assumes that the loss impacts on the team, group and organisation as a whole as well as on individuals.

A particular loss may be publically shared by all or suffered privately by an individual child. Death, especially of a child or staff member, represents an obvious loss, however, other losses need to be recognised. These include losses associated with children and staff who move away, changing friendships, altered self-concept (whether through natural development, ill health, bullying or other abuse) academic and sporting performance, dysfunctional family life, divorce, an absent parent, material or emotional deprivation, and those arising from illness and disability. Unfortunately these are not always recognised as legitimate causes for attention and their impact is diminished by both individuals and the organisation, especially when such losses are experienced by only a few children, perhaps just one.

Parents, families and the wider community may have associated needs and make valuable contributions; however, this chapter deals specifically with the needs of staff and children and the strategies that can be adopted by the organisation when responding to losses experienced by any of its members.

The Impact on Different Types of Organisations and Teams

Before looking at general models of how loss affects organisations and groups and how they respond, it is necessary to be aware of the different contexts in which people work and in which children and staff find themselves. All these variables need to be considered when applying general principles to real-life situations.

Teams always dealing with loss

These include teams where loss is an accepted part of the role. They are usually health-care teams where death and other losses associated with ill health are very much part of the work.

Palliative care teams

In such teams the whole purpose is to support children who are dying. Thus there is no conflict about success only being judged in terms of cure. It is in these teams that many important advances have been made in the care of dying children and their families and in the support of staff. The whole ethos is in the acceptance of loss as a universal force and an inevitable part of life. By this time, children may be over the more traumatic stages of their treatment – or the calm environment of care takes the trauma out of the difficult times.

Emergency and Intensive Therapy Unit teams in hospitals

Although death and other losses happen, the main aim of these teams is to cure. Death is therefore often regarded as failure. They are also likely to see the more traumatic aspects of injury or illness at a time when children and relatives are in a high state of shock. Emergency work staff themselves are likely to be experiencing surges of adrenalin in order to do their task and can suffer a 'low' when it falls. In major incidents, even teams who are used to dealing with horrific death and injury are shocked by the scale of what faces them. Such teams are often not prepared to deal with the impact of loss because it is felt to be such a normal part of their work. Phrases such as 'they should be used to it' or 'they shouldn't be in the job if they aren't' institutionalise such attitudes.

Health-care teams dealing with long-term illness such as Oncology and Haematology Units

These fall between the first two types of team. The aim is to cure, or at least to gain remission, but lessening of the child's quality of life and death are still likely. Relationships may be built up with children and their families over a long period of time. When death comes, the loss can feel very personal to staff. Families are suddenly no longer part of the ward that has become their second home.

Major disaster teams

These include emergency rescue teams (health-care professionals and others) and those responsible for the psychosocial after-care of survivors, the bereaved and the wider disaster community. The development and training of such teams is still relatively new and not always adequate. Few, if any, such teams have survived involvement in major disaster without psychological casualties amongst team members, managers and their families.

Social work teams

These include teams dealing with adoption or placing children with foster parents and those involved with cases of child abuse, disability and recurring socio-economic loss.

Teams not usually dealing with loss

Dealing with children experiencing loss is less frequent and not the main purpose of the work, undertaken by these teams.

Health-care teams

These include teams who work with conditions less likely to result in loss and death, such as maternity teams and community health teams in GP practices. Despite the nature of their work such teams are often not prepared because death is not seen frequently enough to be a priority and the impact of other losses is not always recognised.

Schools and some social service agencies

These organisations exist for purposes not primarily related to death and other losses. Here loss and death are often seen as an intrusion, and sometimes an inconvenience, to what is deemed to be the normal work of the team. Strong feelings may be aroused in team members about whether or not their organisation has any role to play in dealing with loss in children or staff. Once awareness is raised about loss issues, they are found to be more common in such organisations than was realised.

Specialist support and / or self-help groups

These include organisations such as Cancer Care Charities and the Samaritans who deal with particular medical conditions or social situations and the losses that can arise. Some of the organisations, such as The Compassionate Friends or CRUSE – Bereavement Care, deal with bereavement brought about by death. The impact on these teams will depend very much on the quality of selection of staff or volunteers, the resources available for staff support, and the previous experience individuals have of loss and death. Often people are attracted to such groups because of their own losses. This may give them extra experience in dealing with other people's losses, but it can also be detrimental to the individual and team if they are unaware of their own unresolved issues and are unprepared when these are triggered by their work.

The Impact of Loss on Organisations

The ripple effect

When loss hits an organisation, group or family, attention tends to focus on how individual members are faring. The most intense focus falls on those who appear to be most obviously involved or affected.

In this scenario, it is easy for people who are less obviously affected or who do not show their emotions to miss out on care and concern. It is also easy for those who are not comfortable with emotional reactions to polarise people into emotional and weak or controlled and strong. One or two people can thereby carry all the emotional impact for the rest of the team. This role is exhausting, but it is also exhausting for people continually to hide or deny their emotions.

Where people are working together as a team, if one person is affected by an event the repercussions will ripple through the rest of the group. The breadth and depth of this ripple effect will depend on:

- the scale and nature of the event – the larger, the more horrific and extraordinary the event, the greater the ripples, especially if there is anyone to be blamed;
- what has led up to the event;
- what else is happening in the team or organisation, especially if it is causing stress;
- the previous experiences of the team or organisation and the timing of the event in its history, e.g. where several incidents happened in quick succession;
- the personalities, previous experiences, and present emotional state of individuals involved;
- how the event and aftermath is managed by the organisation.

Mass loss, suicide, the loss of a person of special significance to the group, loss as a result of negligence are all likely to trigger a big team reaction. If these occur at the same time as the team is going through other stress, either personal or organisational, then the ripple is exacerbated (Capewell, 1993).

The mechanism for this ripple effect has been described by Johnson (1993) from his work in schools, but it can equally well be applied to all kinds of groups – work teams, families, organisations and communities. It states that any group evolves its own character and level of cohesiveness according to its needs. Less cohesive groups allow for more individuality, more cohesive groups give greater support and group identity. Bonding forces are always competing against forces of fragmentation and divergent interests to produce the level of solidarity. Figure 5.1 illustrates the three stages in a group following incidents which test out the strength of its bonds.

Stage 1: recoil

Immediately after the impact of an event, the group swings rapidly from an initial state of disorganisation to one of fusion when old

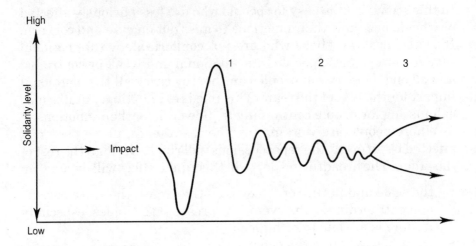

Fig. 5.1 The impact of loss on groups: 1, recoil; 2, reorganisation; 3, restabilisation. (Adapted from Johnson, 1993.)

animosities are forgotten and everyone pulls together for support or to 'defeat' the crisis.

Stage 2: reorganisation

Reorganisation of the group can take place over weeks, months or years. It involves three factors:

- the new conditions, realities and forced change that loss always brings;
- the group's capacity for great solidarity and fusion discovered in Stage 1;
- the re-emergence of old animosities and disputes in the group, fuelled by the exhaustion and stress of the traumatic incident and its consequent changes.

The strength of each factor fluctuates more rapidly than before until it finally settles into a new stability.

Stage 3: restabilisation

The group, if it has survived, now finds a new level of solidarity and establishes new group rules, alliances and norms. If the crisis has had any impact, the group rarely emerges unchanged. Its level of cohesiveness is usually at a higher or lower level than before, rarely the same.

Responses of Organisations to Loss and Grief

Observations and models

The following models are an attempt to make sense in general terms of how organisations respond to loss and grief and the change that these bring. The models broadly correspond to the degree of awareness, training and preparation in relation to loss and grief in an organisation. They seek to draw out common themes and outcomes, remembering of course that a model is a map and not the whole territory.

No response

In Model 1 (Fig. 5.2), the organisation has little or no awareness of the impact of loss on the staff or children. This is most likely to happen where the primary task of the organisation has nothing to do with loss, death and dying or where little attention is given to staff training or support. Children and staff will be expected to fit in with the ethos of the organisation, and services will be geared to what the organisation is prepared to offer rather than what best serves the needs of its members. In this model such events will be seen as the responsibility of the people concerned, not of the organisation.

When a significant loss incident impacts on this kind of organisation, a wall of resistance springs up rapidly. The organisation is so

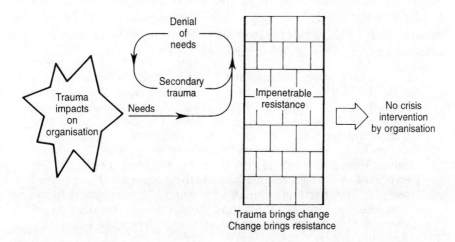

Fig. 5.2 Organisational response to loss. Model 1: no response.

threatened or fearful of the impact or so ill-equipped to deal with it, that it would rather ignore the event than attempt a response. If any response is made, it will be to refer those in need to other agencies. An organisation can be so dysfunctional that though it recognises the serious impact of an incident, it is quite unable to respond appropriately because its normal systems and leadership are in serious disarray.

Unfortunately, such trauma cannot so easily be dismissed by the staff and children who are involved. Rebuttal and non-recognition of their experience will set in motion a process of secondary reactions and suppression of needs and feelings. These may emerge later as depression, aggression and maladaptive behaviour towards the organisation or society in general. Staff and children will receive the message that emotions are not valid or worthy of receiving help. They may not dare to show how they are reacting to others and begin to avoid social contact or situations which remind them of their stress. They may feel isolated, low in self-worth and think they are 'going crazy'. Children are prone to this when adults are always putting on a brave face. The false brightness of others serves to emphasise the fact that they feel so awful and increase feelings of inadequacy that they can't get out of their pit so easily. In schools and other children's institutions, complete denial also means that the opportunity to learn about loss, grief and coping skills will be missed, depriving them of useful knowledge for the future. The taboos of loss and grief will be reinforced.

If such repression and denial comes after a major incident or a series of losses which challenge the structures, culture and cohesiveness of the team or organisation, then the hidden stress has the power to eat quietly away, like an invisible worm, at the psychosocial fabric of the system. It eventually manifests in poor morale, absenteeism, illness, and inefficiency.

> In one organisation dealing with children, within a few months of an incident, a high proportion of the staff had stress-related illnesses causing a higher than usual rate of absenteeism. The organisation was particularly hit when the clerical staff succumbed to stress. When it was also hit by an increase of aggression from children and parents and a spate of burglaries for several months from the time of the incident, the staff began to feel persecuted. A senior manager had a history of personal unresolved losses and had been quite unable to respond appropriately to the workplace incident, denying that there was any need to do so. Unfortunately, those able to intervene directively did not choose to use this power.

Unplanned response

Model 2 (Fig. 5.3) illustrates how an organisation responds when the event is not denied but where there has been no preparation for dealing with loss and grief. As always, trauma and change induce the wall of resistance. The resulting denial of feelings causes some of the secondary reactions described in the first model. But this time the barriers can be by-passed or penetrated, with or without the blessing of the senior managers, and often 'undercover'. Such interventions for staff and children will be unplanned, unco-ordinated, unresourced, ad-hoc and short-term. Staff who inter-vene do so in addition to their normal duties and are unlikely to receive adequate support or recognition from managers and col-leagues. Middle managers and staff who interface with children, parents and the wider community are particularly vulnerable to stress. They are very aware of the emotional needs of staff and children requiring rapid responses, but have to meet them with the procedures of slow-moving bureaucracies (Capewell, 1992, 1993). Those staff and children whose reactions are delayed may be too late to receive help which could only be offered while the incident was still fresh in people's awareness.

This stage is often necessary in order for managers to understand how the impact of loss and grief ripples through the system. But its main characteristic – the polarisation of attitudes – causes major problems. Where the organisation has no agreed policies and staff are unprepared and untrained, there will be many opinions and prejudices about the right and wrong ways of responding to both

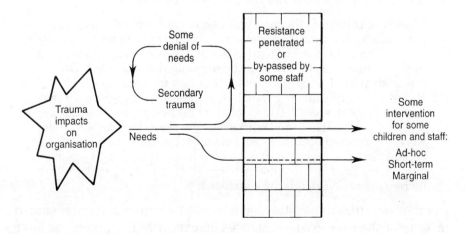

Fig. 5.3 Organisational response to loss. Model 2: unplanned response.

children and staff. A rapid polarisation has been observed into interventionist and non-interventionist camps, between the stiff upper-lip brigade and those who believe feelings should be recognised and may be expressed. This is a time- and energy-consuming process, full of damaging judgements and labels about who is strong and weak. It exposes all the other differences and issues that people have about the system, which are tolerated in non-stressful times.

Children and colleagues in need of help will also gravitate to those staff who they sense are more sympathetic to their needs. This means that some staff believe that everyone is alright while the others become overburdened in trying to help so many people. A great deal of anger, criticism and scapegoating can fly between the opposing camps. A strong manager is needed who is not afraid to be directive during the crisis period and who can keep above the splits and unite the various factions. Too often the manager strongly identifies with a particular side. Unfortunately, a good non-crisis manager may not be a good crisis manager, and lack of preparation means that the work cannot easily be delegated. Often the least-expected member of staff emerges as a real leader in times of stress.

The outcome for the organisation can be serious as the health of the staff team becomes mirrored in the health of the service and children. This is especially so in schools and children's homes where they spend so much time together. Disunity and splits among the overt authority figures lead to voids which are in danger of being filled by the covert authority figures such as the school or home bullies, or a particularly dominant group of staff.

> In one organisation, the manager had never been able to control a particularly dominant group of staff who had been in post for many years. Elements of the critical incident had been very challenging to their beliefs about the way the organisation operated. During the crisis period, they criticised any action the manager took and stated strongly that any member of staff who sought help was 'weak'. They denied that any of the children were affected and resented external help and advice. During the following year, there were unexpected staff resignations and illness; at the end of the second year, the manager took early retirement on health grounds, having suffered a breakdown because of the dominant group's increasing pressure after the incident.

In other organisations, staff have become burnt-out, have resigned in spite of the severe consequences on career and finances, or have remained full of anger and bitterness which seeps out into their relationships with other members of the team. Some have turned to alcohol, drugs or crime, and a few suicides have been recorded. Much suffering can remain undetected for years until another stressful incident occurs.

The planned response

Model 3 (Fig. 5.4) illustrates the responses most likely at present to be found in organisations such as hospices where the whole ethos encompasses a healthy attitude towards loss and grief. The need for opportunities for staff, children and their families to deal positively and openly with their reactions is accepted and understood.

In this model, the need to prepare for dealing with loss and grief throughout the organisation and in relation to services offered to staff, children, their families and the wider community is understood. It is accepted and therefore legitimised as part of the normal role of the organisation. Resources have been allocated to preparation, implementation and training well before a significant loss occurs. When it does, no time and energy is wasted in arguments or long debates on the need to respond or on how to respond. Roles, procedures, options and communication systems have already been implemented and tested. Staff have sufficient understanding and training to be able to apply the plans flexibly to meet the specific needs of the situation. External help will be valued as much as the internal resources and used appropriately.

Because planning and training has involved the whole organisation, unhelpful resistant attitudes will have been dispelled or contained. They will not be dominant enough to prevent staff or children having their needs recognised and met. A full range of co-ordinated interventions will be possible in an environment of

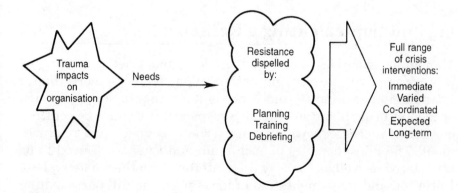

Fig. 5.4 Organisational response to loss. Model 3: planned response.

support and care, free from the fear of judgements and labels, and staff will be supported. Learning will be gathered from the response without the need to be defensive about mistakes. The feedback will influence future responses. Children will have experienced good adult models for coping and dealing with loss. They will have had the opportunity to learn lessons which will stay with them for life. Staff and children will feel empowered. The outcome for the organisation will be an increased morale and self-worth leading to greater cohesion. This will have a positive and long-term effect on staff and children who are coping with loss and grief.

> In one school, though they had not prepared specifically for loss, the culture was supportive and aware enough for external help to be sought soon after two pupils died in tragic circumstances and within sight of many other pupils. The staff were debriefed and given information and training soon after the event. Two weeks later, they were able to respond with more confidence when another pupil was on a life support machine and had her arm amputated. This time they could discuss issues more openly with the children and work out strategies for preparing them either for the girl's death or her return to school. Luckily she survived and her transition back to school was supported with love, and practical help.

The best examples of planned and co-ordinated responses can be found abroad, though in all cases mentioned, the implementation of the concept has taken a great deal of hard work from a few dedicated people, especially where schools are involved. Excellent work is now done throughout Israeli schools, New York City School Board began the process in 1990, and in 1992 it became mandatory for school Principals in New South Wales, Australia to respond to losses which affect the school community.

Preparing and Implementing a Response

Managing sensitive issues such as loss and grief is a complex process requiring careful implementation. It needs more than a fixed plan or technique, and it needs more than a single decision or idea to bring about an effective response. It requires a continuous set of processes with ongoing review, feedback and readjustment. The idiosyncracies of each team and their work need to be considered as well as the way they interact with the whole system. Initiation and implementation of ideas need the full participation of key staff and all who are involved. Sufficient time especially needs to be given to the early stages of the process. The process itself also needs to be valued as much, if not more than, the finished programme. Figure 5.5 illustrates the process for implementation.

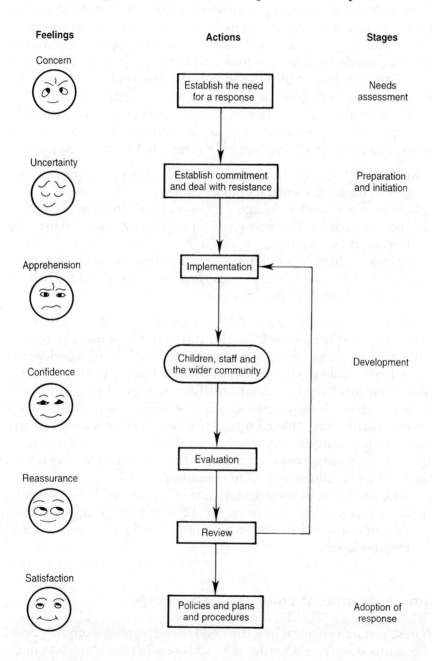

Fig. 5.5 Model for implementing loss and grief responses. (Adapted from R. Heinecke and R. Spence, 'Children and loss', unpublished paper, 1991.)

Assessing the needs

The starting point for any preparation, especially if it involves new ideas, is to find out what happens in the organisation already. This identifies strengths that can be built on and the presence of resistance that needs to be understood and changed. The best solutions grow naturally from what already exists. The scale of change also has to be assessed, bearing in mind that the introduction of the concept of preparing an organisational response to loss and grief will require change of some degree. Golembiewski (1976) provides useful classification of the types of change that may be required:

* alpha or first order change – minor, simple and routine changes such as making a ward feel more homely;
* beta or second order change – changes involving a new working practice such as the introduction of psychological debriefing after a critical incident;
* gamma or third order change – major, fundamental changes to the culture of the team or organisation in which radical shifts occur in values and assumptions.

Alpha changes are most likely to be needed, if at all, in organisations whose culture from the start is holistic and caring and whose primary task includes the support of children experiencing loss and grief. Beta changes are likely where the culture is conducive to loss and grief work, but where there is a need for changes in awareness or working practices, or a need to fulfil health and safety at work regulations regarding staff stress. Gamma changes are especially necessary in organisations which do not have a culture which can contain stress or recognise that loss and grief are issues that need to be addressed. One community health-care team, for example, would not allow a doctor time off to deal with his brother's suicide. Examples for the need for gamma change are found in schools where the culture does not allow a child's loss and grief to be accommodated.

Creating an environment conducive to change

Change is much easier when the needs are accepted from the top of the organisation; much harder when it is not. In the latter case, more subtle strategies from enlightened staff are required in order to bring about change from within or to convince managers of a need which they do not recognise. Often the point of acceptance of an idea comes when the costs of not attending to it are greater than the costs of implementation, especially now that litigation relating to staff stress is increasing.

Because of the existential nature of loss and grief, organisations that can cope with and manage change generally will be in the best position to deal with these issues. These organisations will have a clear organisational vision, task, values and goals; good and reliable systems for consultation, communications and decision making; and procedures that support the task rather than dull creativity. Staff will be selected as the result of sound selection procedures, their roles will be clearly defined and stated, and people will be treated with respect. Minority needs will be respected. There will be an atmosphere of learning from experience rather than fear of doing things differently (Hawkins and Shohet, 1989). Crisis exposes any weaknesses in the system that can be tolerated in normal times. Thus the basis of dealing with loss and grief and especially crisis on a large scale is:

- good quality management;
- effective staff selection and ongoing development;
- good quality organisational development and team building.

If an open and caring environment is created, then it will also be communicated in the way staff operate and behave toward children, their families and each other.

> When my daughter was admitted to the Haematology Unit at the John Radcliffe Hospital in Oxford (now the Oxford Radcliffe Hospital) I was full of anxiety not only about her illness but also about the way she would be dealt with by staff and the system. Many of my anxieties were allayed when I found a notice pinned to the wall of her room clearly stating the Unit's philosophy. Patients and families were clearly seen as partners in the treatment who had individual physical, emotional and spiritual needs and ways of coping that would be respected. It was particularly important that I knew this from the outset without the stress of having to ask. I didn't have to work out what the hidden agenda and values of the Unit were, or worry about what would or would not be acceptable. It was also important that staff practised what they preached. On further investigation, I discovered that before the Unit opened all the staff had been involved in two weeks of team development where they came to a consensus about the values which would guide how they worked. The cycle of learning, review and development continues. The solid foundations on which good practice was built showed in many everyday aspects of life on the ward. Staff did not wear uniforms. The bathroom was nicely decorated and was a place to relax. All staff – doctors, nurses, administrators, cleaners were regarded as having different

but equally valued skills to offer the team. Parents, or indeed anyone, could stay overnight if the patient wished. Brothers, sisters, friends and children were not excluded. Religious and cultural needs were accepted, especially regarding dying and death. On the night my daughter was dying it was quite acceptable for us to turn a very clinical room into a sacred place lit by candles. A nurse could cry and a doctor could meet you in the corridor with a hug. The care continued after the death – staff attended the funeral, invited us back to the ward at any time to ask questions or just for a chat. The spontaneous and human responses meant so much to us and prevented our grief becoming blocked or distorted by bad practices.

Anticipating the resistance

Change always brings resistance, however good the organisation. Some is necessary to keep change grounded in reality. But often it is damaging and is the result of fear of the unknown, poor management or trust, or a sense of threat to status or skills.

The fear of the loss and grief

Fear itself is enough to stop many professionals from even thinking about loss and grief let alone face it enough to deal with it at work. Resistance of this kind is most likely to occur in organisations or teams where their main task is about cure or services for the living.

Personal history of loss and grief in staff

There can be an incredible amount of hidden and disenfranchised grief in staff teams in schools and other caring organisations. It is particularly relevant when the manager has not previously dealt with such losses and, as a result, resists any interventions being made with staff or children. This is also backed by the research carried out in schools in New South Wales (Rowling, 1994) which revealed hidden grief to be one of the major inhibitors to schools implementing planned responses.

In a school team affected by the suicide of a colleague, the staff were paralysed about explaining the death to the children. Talking about death was hard enough, suicide was impossible and taboo. The block was dealt with by the team sharing all they knew about suicide. It soon emerged that nearly everyone had had some experience of suicide, some recently and at close quarters. Other tragic losses in their lives also emerged.

Attitudes and myths about loss and grief and children

When the loss is the death of a child, the impact takes on extra significance because of:

- the challenge that the loss of a child poses to most adults;
- the myths surrounding the distress and grief of children involved in the loss.

Both of these issues have to be considered by organisations preparing a response to loss and grief because they considerably influence attitudes and willingness to intervene in a proactive manner. The challenge to adults is a challenge to their position as protectors of the young and to the faith that the young have in them to prevent awful things happening or to make them better if they do happen. When the loss is a death, it is also a challenge to the perceived natural order of life that the old should die before the young. For those professionals who are not normally dealing with death, as in schools, or in health-care teams where cure is the normal outcome, then the infrequency of such incidents challenge their preparedness and their known skills and coping mechanisms.

Fortunately, the work of professionals who care for seriously ill, dying and bereaved children has done a great deal to disprove many of the myths surrounding children in distress and those who grieve. There is still a long way to go, however, in dispelling these myths in society in general and among many professionals, including those who work with children.

The myths and fears surrounding death and distress involving children include the following.

- Children are more resilient than adults or are not so affected by trauma.
- If children are affected, then they will 'be over it' in a few days.
- Children under seven, and especially those under five, do not understand what is going on so will not be affected and will not need information or help.
- Children who are not showing outward signs of being affected are not affected.
- Mentioning the event or offering help will create problems where there are none.

Institutionalised attitudes

As well as the myths held by individuals, there are also commonly stated institutional attitudes and cliches which help to create an environment which influences the willingness of the organisation to respond to the losses experienced by children and staff. Examples from schools include the following.

- It is not part of our normal role.
- School is a haven from the 'real world'.
- Only the children need help, the teachers do not.
- We must get back to normal immediately (with the implication that the incident should be forgotten or not mentioned after a short period of time).
- We have a wonderful pastoral – care system (with the implication that external help is not required).
- The child does not need or deserve help because it is the 'neurotic mother creating the problem' or the child had problems before.

Children and adolescents who are deemed to be trouble makers or who are socially unnacceptable may also be excluded from sympathetic treatment by prejudicial attitudes.

Salter (1990) has drawn attention to the statements, myths and metaphors made within the health-care and local government systems following the Lockerbie disaster, which prevented staff from receiving help and support. Many staff will talk about their emotional reactions 'off-the record' but clam up as soon as they are part of their professional team. Teachers expressing concern for the emotional state of pupils are also fearful of being seen as 'soft' or as making excuses for their pupils by their more task-orientated or less emotionally aware peers.

The professional's need to be in control

In many professions, great store has been traditionally set on the professional being seen to be in control. Loss and grief experienced by children, especially when this involves the death of a child, challenges this belief that adults can always be in control. Some, especially those in management roles, respond by retreating into bureaucracy, applying rigid procedures and rules more fervently; others become over – involved with the pain of the children. The fears created by the possibility of loss of control and therefore chaos may also be displaced outwards. Children are easy receptacles for this and may be labelled as the ones who are distressed or in need. It is easier for some adults to define a child as being in need rather than dealing with their own needs. Where the professionals are responsible for large groups of children it is not surprising that they are afraid of mass hysteria breaking out if a loss is mentioned at all.

Removing the barriers

With such a sensitive issue as loss, time and energy must be given to dealing with resistance so that the work will not be sabotaged. The commitment must always come from within but it is often necessary to involve external consultants and trainers to mobilise staff. They are able to provide the safety for staff to expose their fears and anxieties because they are not their managers or colleagues. Three strategies are especially important for dealing with resistance.

- *Education*: in initial professional training; through in-service and external courses; and personal/team review, learning and supervision.
- *Staff care and support*: within the team and through formal staff care systems or employee assistance programmes.
- *Management strategies*: policies, plans, procedures which are well implemented and mean that the work is part of normal procedures.

In an ideal world, the more society opens up discussion about loss and death, taking on spiritual and emotional issues as well as intellectual ones, resistance will be less of a problem. Schools, colleges and universities have an important role to play here, as do educational institutions involved in preparing professional carers.

Developing and planning a response

The elements of a good response broadly include interventions *before, during and after* an incident for both staff and children. In relation to children these will usually involve multi-agency strategies for which cross-agency discussions, planning and training are required, especially where the aims and values of agencies differ. All too often this is neglected, leading to confusion. Hospitals, for example, may be aiming for a quick throughput of patients, while community social service and health -care teams may feel more time is needed, either for emotional issues to be handled or while they arrange adequate care at home. Children can also miss out on services such as bereavement support because no team is clear about who should be dealing with this and liaison is poor.

Using Caplan's classification of types of intervention (Caplan, 1964), responses can include the following.

Pre-incident preventive education programmers.

- For staff: loss and grief education and training.
- For children: loss and death, peer support, coping skills programmes in schools; health education programmes about loss and grief and stress management.

Crisis intervention during or immediately after an incident

- For staff: mobilisation of crisis plan; on-site defusing using short interventions designed to defuse intense emotions in the team and directive leadership to remove staff who need a break or who become too affected by the trauma; full critical incident stress debriefing for the most stressful incidents.
- For children: providing information, alternatives, practical support proactively; practices which reduce or do not increase their stress, e.g. respecting personal preferences and religious and cultural conventions.

Therapeutic / rehabilitative interventions

- For staff: screening/counselling for individual staff with long-term reactions; team rebuilding for major incidents or after loss of a team member.
- For children: ensuring that someone is responsible for giving information about support services; giving post-trauma information or debriefing as a preventive measure before problems arise; keeping the lines of communication open for long enough to pick up on delayed reactions remembering that time gets distorted after loss, especially for children.

In organisations not normally dealing with loss, interventions may only be offered after the incident, though even these are still uncommon. These are fraught with difficulty as no one knows what to expect and insufficient time and resources are allocated. All kinds of stresses arise in staff at such times. As a consultant, I have found myself being expected to deal with past personal traumas, everyday stresses of working in a particular profession, and detailed issues about individual staff and children as well as the aftermath of the incident and the questions these raise for people who have not considered them before. Such pressures can be reduced if some of these issues are addressed beforehand.

Structures and procedures

These must grow naturally out of the process described. The nature of the team and its work will require different solutions. Whatever structure evolves, it must be simple, flexible, understood by everyone and be part of the induction for new staff, practised regularly, and be regularly reviewed. It must also be workable even if the team leader is absent. Many big disasters occur out of working hours, in holiday times and across administrative borders.

For small teams working constantly with loss, their response has to be firmly built in to everyday practice. External supervisors and team consultants may be needed to give objectivity and renewal to the team at regular intervals and after particularly stressful events. Where loss and grief are not so frequently experienced, then it may not be appropriate for everyone to be fully trained. All staff should be aware of organisational policies and the help they can expect following incidents. They should also receive enough information and training to give them confidence in handling colleagues, children and families affected by loss. In schools for example, a lot of damage is done by teachers who dismiss or minimise the significance of the loss (particularly likely when this is not related to a death) do not understand how the child's reactions may be affecting school performance and behaviour, and take action (or no action) which increases the child's stress. In such organisations, a special crisis or loss and grief team can be established to receive more intensive training and preparation. They can act as a resource group for the rest of the staff.

In large organisations, the team can be drawn from within, receiving external help for large scale incidents. In smaller organisations, one or two people can be drawn from several in an area to form a joint specialist team. In New York City, District Crisis Response Teams serve clusters of schools. Their members are a mix of teachers, administrators and school psychologists, and they have regular training and review from external experts. Capewell (1994) provides a full account of structures for schools.

The East Wiltshire Health Care Trust provides a good example of a structure designed to cope with many different needs and teams. The Staff Support Service is a confidential service available to all National Health Service staff and covers hospital- and community-based teams. Its success is due to the enlightenment of managers, the skills and insight of the co-ordinator who implemented and developed the service, and the timing. The initial idea for the project had just been put forward when the Swindon hospitals became the recipients for the victims of the Hungerford shootings in 1987. The characteristics of this incident meant that the impact on the staff was immense, even though many were used to dealing with horrific injuries. The need for having a planned response for dealing with casualties, their families, and the staff was high-lighted and gave the impetus to develop the Staff Support Service. Not only does the Service deal with individual staff it also acts as a catalyst on the wards and in other teams for better staff training and team building. Its reputation is such that it is also working with other agencies such as schools.

Key Points

For individual staff

- Begin preparing for loss and grief *now* – it can strike *now*.
- Don't stop – preparing never ends.
- Listen and learn from those affected and give them professional responses in a human manner.
- Learn to value the expression of feelings as a positive method of coping and communicating, rather than as a sign of weakness.
- Do not deny your own pain of loss and grief – this is your greatest resource for being able to be with others in pain.
- Learn to view loss as a natural part of life so even death can be approached positively.
- Take responsibility for yourself in the organisation – it's not all down to management.

For teams

- Build the team as a container that can support distress.
- Continual redevelopment – especially after each loss situation.
- Learn to acknowledge everyday endings and 'losses' in the team – farewells, retirements.

For organisations

- Take a proper management responsibility for supporting teams and individuals.
- Create a culture and environment which cares for staff – they'll pass it on to others.
- Creating good administrative structures which support the work and providing the physical resources needed for the job is half the solution.
- The other half is in the training and support of staff – all grades and positions.
- Value training for attitudes and process as much as cognitive- and task-orientated subjects.
- Avoid tokenism – staff and especially children easily discern genuine responses.

Conclusion

Planning a good response for staff and children requires time, commitment and sensitivity. It is a partnership between the managers of the organisation, the teams set up to achieve its goals, and all of the individuals who make up the team and organisation. Each must take some responsibility for preparing for this work. A few saboteurs in strategic roles can render all plans and preparations useless. But if all are working together, then the benefits can be seen in reduction of stress in staff and children, less harrowing grief in those who have suffered loss, and some very positive experiences in spite of the difficulties of the loss situation.

These all have cost benefits too in terms of reduced costs of staff illness, inefficiency, sabotage, absenteeism, alcholism and other maladaptive behaviours. Early grief and trauma interventions also reduce subsequent visits to GPs and help children regain their previous skills and school performance (Yule and Gold, 1993). Costs to society are also reduced if grieving parents are able to return to work, if traumatised children do not have their psychological growth inhibited, if organisations are not weakened by stress and trauma, and if everyone from an early age begins to view loss more positively because they are not afraid to face the issues and have learnt the skills of coping for life.

References

Capewell, E. (1992) The clash of the gods. *Association of Counselling at Work*, June: 14.

Capewell, E. (1993) Responding to the needs of young people after hungerford. In T. Newburn (Ed.), *Working with Disaster – Social Welfare Interventions During and After Tragedy*. Harlow: Longman.

Capewell, E. (1994) Systems for managing critical incidents in Schools. Report, Centre for Crisis Management and Education, Newbury.

Caplan, G. (1964) *Principles of Preventive Psychiatry*. New York: Basic Books.

Golembiewski, R.T. (1976) *Learning and Change in Groups*. London: Penguin.

Hawkins, P. and Shohet, R. (1989) *Supervision in the Helping Professions*. Milton Keynes: Open University Press.

Johnson, K. (1993) *School Crisis Management*. Alameda, California: Hunter House.

Rowling, L. (1994) Loss and grief in the health promoting school. Thesis, University of Southampton.

Salter, D. (1990) Lockerbie and after – myths and metaphors. *Changes*, **8**: 311.

Yule, W. and Gold, A. (1993) *Wise Before the Event*. London: Calouste Gulbenkian Foundation.

6
Long Term Follow-Up and Support

Penny Cook

This chapter explores the long-term support of children after loss. Being able to recognise a grieving child, understanding difficulties in grieving, talking with parents and ideas for them to help the children are discussed. For most children, grief is a normal reaction to a loss and specialist or so called expert advice is not needed. What *is* needed is for the child to be understood and to be heard, so it is essential for the adults to be able to do this naturally. Issues around the long-term illness and death of a sibling or parent are considered, as are childrens' feelings, involvement, changing needs, and death in school.

Finally, ways of helping children include some thoughts on support groups, specialised help and what may be available locally.

> A child can live through anything so long as he or she is told the truth and is allowed to share with loved ones the natural feelings people have when they are suffering (Le Shan, 1976)

Adults often feel unable to help grieving children. They may consider themselves inadequate through lack of experience or knowledge, or they may not have the confidence to talk naturally with children they feel are vulnerable and for whom they want to 'get it right'. They may want to protect the child from the pain of talking about the loss or be afraid of their own reactions to tears, distress or bad feelings.

As a result many children are not given honest information and opinions. The use of euphemisms and avoidance of certain subjects adds to the confusion and increases the risk of long-term problems.

It is not, therefore, surprising that for many children, the pain and difficulties of grieving are not recognised or shared. They may even take years to resolve. A grieving child may be surrounded at home by family and friends who are also grieving, and this loss of the normal family adds to the insecurity. Useful support is needed from other adults who are trusted by the child, but perhaps are not emotionally involved in the family crisis. The long-term support of these children should, perhaps, be a continuation and natural progression of the care given earlier (if possible) and at the time of the loss. This calls for good communication and co-ordination between the carers and health care professional involved with the family. Those involved might include the palliative care team, hospital nurses, general practitioners, social workers, chaplains, play specialists, psychologists, counsellors, school nurses, health visitors, family therapists and teachers.

Before adults can begin to help children with their grieving they must have addressed certain issues for themselves. These include their own thoughts, experiences, feelings and fears. There may be some unresolved grief from childhood losses, which prevents them from being totally open to what a child brings to them. It may not feel safe to be in touch with the bereaved child within themselves and this prevents a deeper relationship with the child.

It would seem sensible preparation for everyone working with children to learn about the stages of children's understanding of death and of their expected reactions to loss. The most important skills are to be able to listen and to enable children to talk. These grow naturally from basic human warmth and compassion.

Bereavement education begins in childhood by talking about the normal losses in life, as they happen. The death of a pet, loss of a favourite toy, even a friend who moves away can be a valuable learning experience if handled appropriately by the family. The teacher who encourages a child to tell the class about the death of a pet hamster is helping all the children in the class to learn about dying and how we feel about it. The children begin to learn that dying is normal and that it is something about which they can talk. Wells (1988) agrees that a teacher's most important job is not to wait for a tragedy to occur, but to talk with children about death whenever the opportunity arises.

When we consider the long-term support of children who have lost someone or something important it could be helpful to look back to past experiences to see how they may help in understanding and managing what is happening now. For example, ask if they remember that the dead goldfish looked just like a goldfish, but that it could not swim or eat any more and that it did not come alive again. It is worth finding out how the family deal with a crisis – are the children involved in discussions, or are they left out, confused and afraid to ask questions.

Children need to grieve, just as adults do; they need to know who or what they have lost and how and why it has been lost. From this they move on to living with the loss, realising what this means for them and trying to make sense of the loss. There may be a painfully difficult period before the child feels secure enough to adapt to the changed situation.

Worden (1984) has identified clear tasks of mourning:

- accepting the reality of the loss;
- experiencing the pain and grief;
- adjusting to the environment in which the dead person is absent;
- reinvesting in new relationships.

These are major necessary achievements for children, just as they are for adults in the journey through grief.

Difficulties in Grieving

There can be many problems. Grieving may be delayed or postponed, especially if it does not seem to be allowed, when, for example no one else may be crying or talking about feelings. There may also be a refusal to accept the loss, perhaps because they do not want to believe it or because there does not seem to be enough evidence to make it seem real.

There may be pressure from other, often older relatives for the child to be 'brave'; 'do not upset Mum by letting her see you cry', 'you must be the strong one now'. If only the adults would acknowledge the child's sadness and allow time for them to all cry together.

The child may not have been given truthful information and still be needing to know what has really happened. The frequent use of euphemisms does not help. It only seems to add to confusion and a sense of isolation.

> Four-year-old Zoe overheard her mother talking with a lady who said they had just lost their baby. Zoe asked if she could help the lady look for her baby – a perfectly reasonable suggestion from a child who could not be expected to understand the baby had died.
>
> Richard was five years old when his grandfather died, and he was told that Jesus had taken him away in his sleep, to live with him in heaven. Richard became afraid of going to sleep, especially with his bedroom window open, in case he too would be taken away in his sleep. When he asked where heaven was, he was told it was in the sky. When his father went on a business trip by air he became very upset; planes fly in the sky, heaven is in the sky – will Daddy be coming back?

If adults do not know the answers they should say so, there is no shame in sharing the truth with a child. The feeling of trust will also be reinforced when the child realises that if adults do not know the answers they will say so and that there may not be answers to everything.

Anger may emerge from even the most placid of children and needs to be handled carefully. It is quite natural to feel angry after a loss, but a child may be frightened by the powerful feelings. Talking about the loss helps to defuse the fear and provide appropriate direction for the fear.

Children can be so frightened of dying or suffering the same fate that they dare not think about what has happened. They may also develop a real fear of losing their parents or carers, leading to considerable anxiety or panic at separation times such as going to bed or school.

Even young children can feel responsible for events and other people's actions. They may carry a huge burden of guilt, believing that somehow they should have done something to save a person or prevent something happening.

However hard it may be for adults struggling with their own emotions, it is so important to remember that the children of a family are also facing a loss. Appropriate preparation and involvement of children before and at the time of the loss is usually a significant part of long-term help. New and multiple losses may even add to the burden of grief and may slow the progress of adjustment.

Some of the common losses faced by children are given in the list below. Some are relatively smaller than others, but they could prove devastating to a child who is already grieving.

- Family: new brother or sister;
           separation of parents;
           death of a grandparent or other relative;
           loss of employment by a parent;
           moving home;
           death of a pet.
- School: starting school;
           changing school;
           change of teacher;
           bullying;
           poor results;
           leaving school.
- Medical: illness;
           loss of movement or function (e.g. broken leg);
           hospital admission;
           hospital visit.
- Personal: loss of a favourite game or toy;
           friend who moves away;
           change in body image (e.g. haircut or scar).

Recognizing Signs of Grieving

If other family members are suffering with their grief they may not be able to notice changes in a child's behaviour. It is often a teacher, health visitor, friend or nurse who does. In any case the family should be aware of possible reactions and be able to discuss them with an experienced person. This emphasises the importance of informing the school when a child is bereaved or experiences any trauma or change in lifestyle.

Children often become unusually quiet or withdrawn. They may be afraid to ask questions or feel unable to talk to anyone at home so that the anger, guilt and sadness build up inside, leading to despair and depression. It is possible that simple things such as a lack of concentration may be noticed by the teacher or play group leader. At home, they may forget where they put things or not pay attention to stories and television programmes. They may appear to wander aimlessly and stare into space. Nailbiting, twiddling strands of hair and finger sucking may increase.

The attitude to food and meal times may change; some children will lose their appetite and interest in food which they normally enjoy, while others may just eat for the sake of eating at any time. It is as if eating fills the empty space inside – 'comfort eating'.

Bedtimes should be a time for extra love and attention. Fears of being alone, particularly in the dark, staying awake for long spells before sleep and possibly nightmares may last for many months and even years. Phobias about anything to do with the loss, such as doctors, hospitals, men and travelling in cars may also develop.

Children, like adults, may also develop psychosomatic responses to loss, for example, tummy pains, sickness, diarrhoea and vague pains in limbs or joints. A general lethargy and lowered resistance to infections may increase the frequency of colds, ear infections and other minor ailments. Regression to an earlier stage of development is common when suffering distress or insecurity. This may show as not eating lumpy food, wanting to be fed, talking baby language, bed wetting, soiling of pants and other baby-like features such as thumb sucking and needing help with dressing.

This change in behaviour can add to the parents' sense of hopelessness. Regular reassurance may be needed to restore their confidence as capable parents.

Talking with Parents

The child's parents may also be grieving and their feelings need to be acknowledged. Perhaps they could be helped by talking to an understanding friend, a counsellor from CRUSE Bereavement Care, a minister of religion or a support organisation.

It would be important to look at how their grief is affecting the children. This may not be easy when they are engulfed in their own strong emotions. The parents may be hiding behind the children and say that they are all right, but are worried about the children. They may also develop a kind of dependence on the children and say how wonderful they have been, which increases pressure on the children to be 'wonderful' all the time. Some guidance on expected behaviour changes and how these may be managed are usually appreciated.

The following list of ideas for parents to help children with their grief was written by Compassionate Friends, (1989, reprinted with permission):

General ideas

1) The first thing to communicate to the child is 'You are not alone, I am with you.'
2) Share feelings with children. They want and need information

and participation in the grief process. (Often parents wish to protect children from the reality, seeing it as a time of innocence.)

3) Let children know that feelings take precedence – stop cooking, reading the paper etc.

4) Make sure that children get the clear message that the death was not their fault. It was not because they were bad in any way or because they were unlovable. Neither was there anything they could have done or can still do to change the situation.

5) Do not tell the child 'Don't worry' or 'Don't be sad' etc. As with parental grief, they are unable to control their responses. Also, avoid messages that tell the child what he or she should or should not be feeling. Do not criticise or seem shocked by statements and feelings.

6) Encourage the child to accept strong feelings, explaining that recovery to creative healthy living involves pain. Unfortunately, there is no short cut.

7) Be honest about the deceased and show that they were loved for themselves alone, with all their strengths and weaknesses. Let children know their *value* has not changed and that they are still *loved* and *special*..

8) Do not deny your pain. It is all right to cry in front of your child.

9) The child may speak of feeling the presence of the dead person. Do not dismiss this lightly because some children, like some adults do have these experiences.

10) Do not say the dead child 'fell asleep and did not wake up'.

11) Do not say 'we lost our child' as children will fear becoming lost while out shopping etc.

12) Take care of your marriage. It is easy to neglect other members of the family at times of loss.

13) Parent-teacher co-operation should be sought. Teachers underestimate the time that a child may be disorganised. It usually lasts beyond the first anniversary of the death.

14) Do not worry about 'regression'. Allow it until equilibrium and energies are renewed. The child usually emerges stronger and more competent. If the regressive behaviour causes problems away from the home try asking the child to confine the behaviour to the home and explain the reasons for the request.

15) To increase confidence, encourage the child in all his/her abilities.

Practical ideas

1) Many children will respond to physical comfort. Suggestions are:

    a) Give special foods. Soft foods can be reassuring and are a reminder of earlier, easier times.

    b) Children respond to snuggling against a warm, soft rough surface, so let them sleep between flannelette sheets or have a blanket on top of them.

    c) Extra clothes in daytime help reduce the coldness of shock and instils a feeling of being lovingly wrapped and protected against possible harm.

2) If difficulty in settling to sleep for relaxation, allow a radio or tape to play softly.

3) For fear of the dark, use a night light.

4) Children need physical play. Try not to cut this time down, even if the child is getting behind with school work owing to a lack of concentration. Seek teacher participation.

5) Grief is tiring so alternate a child's passive and active occupations. Arrange a quiet time in the afternoon and plan an early bedtime.

6) If they are having difficulty following directions make lists. These can be done in pictures for the very young.

7) A special outing, treat or present or colourful clothing can bring comfort and help to create a feeling of security.

8) If a child is over-eating serve the food on individual plates. You could say 'I wonder if you are really hungry, lets try a cuddle instead'.

9) Offer small nourishing meals to those who have lost interest in eating.

10) For both over-eating and under-eating, teach the child to cook.

These suggestions are sensible advice for those helping children with any loss, crisis or change in their way of life.

Long Term Illness of a Parent

It is often difficult enough to maintain a reasonably normal routine for children when a parent is ill for a few days, such as during 'flu or while recovering from an injury, so a long-term illness can be very traumatic. For most children there is security in familiar surroundings and a regular routine. When parents are not able to continue this the children will be affected by the loss of what they know as normal. Anxieties develop and grow into fears of what may happen. In these circumstances they need:

- *Reassurance* that – they will be cared for and not be left alone. If it is necessary to leave them for a while it is important that they are left with people whom they know and trust. The doctors and nurses are doing everything to help the sick parent – making him or her comfortable, stopping pain, and trying to make them better. It is good for them to meet and talk to these people themselves.
- *Information*, which should be given correctly and simply according to the age and understanding of the child. If children are not given facts they imagine them, often creating a picture rather different from the real one. There may be a genuine fear that the parent might die and whether or not this is realistic the child needs to share the thoughts. It does seem only fair for children to know why they are spending more time with relations and friends and why mummy or daddy is in hospital.

Involving Children

Children like to be involved, to be part of what is going on around them and there are usually ways in which they can feel helpful. Around the home they can fetch and carry for a sick or disabled parent and help with the care, such as brushing hair or feeding. Being helpful need not be the only way to be involved. There are other ways of sharing which are good for the child and good for the sick parent. Denial and pretence can create barriers which prevent natural and normal sharing. Simple pleasures, such as sharing a chair or a bed to watch a favourite television programme together or read a story would be therapeutic to both.

There may be a risk that the adults in the family expect too much from the children. They may be expected to be good at all times, to keep out of the way and to help with an increasing number of chores. The children will need time to do normal activities when possible and not be made to feel guilty when they are having fun. The familiar routine of school provides a structure to the days and weeks and a diversion from some uncertainty or sadness at home. Physical activity is also an outlet for pent up energy and frustrations and the chance for social development with other children.

As a death comes close, children should be given the chance to say goodbye. If they are not given the choice, there may be serious resentment and regrets even many years later.

Death of a Parent

For some children, the death of a parent is one more stressful event after many. For others it is traumatic or sudden. For them all it is the end of life the way it was, it cannot be the same again.

Adaption to a life without that parent involves making a new relationship with the missing person and being comfortable and comforted by memories. The ways children cope and survive for the future depend on many factors including their own natural ability and resilience and how they have coped with previous losses, but they all need time to mourn. Fourteen-year-old Joanne was angry when her father died: 'My Dad didn't deserve to die, he was too good, too young'. No adult could dispute that.

When talking to adults who were children or adolescents when a parent died or became separated from them, the memories are often clear. Anger and resentment are strong when they had not been included, when nobody had told them what was happening.

The changed relationship with the remaining parent, the possible new partner, the level of support and understanding from family, friends, peer group and school are all important factors.

The remaining parent is grieving and the family has changed. If grandparents are alive they will also be mourning the loss of their child and yet perhaps trying to take on part of that role in caring for the children.

There will be fears of separation from the parent and for their safety. An older child will often show great concern if the surviving parent is late home, fearing a car accident. Even young children become protective, like six-year-old Graham who solemnly told his mother that he would look after her as Daddy was not coming home any more. He thought he was so big and strong, but within a few minutes he had climbed on to Mummy's lap for a cuddle and a suck of his thumb.

The family dynamics will change; members may take on different roles and responsibilities. Children need reassurance that someone is going to care for them – provide foods or earn money, take them to football or Brownies. Three-year-old Oliver made his own decision to call his auntie Sarah 'Mummy Sarah' after the sudden death of his mother and father. He went to live with this aunt who provided for and cared for him in place of his mother.

Older children may be forced by circumstances to take on more domestic chores and shopping. These new responsibilities may be hard to fit around schoolwork.

Long-Term Illness of a Sibling

The brothers and sisters of a chronic or terminally ill child are often forced to take a back seat when the sibling needs constant attention. Children have been heard to say that they wished they had cancer because you get lots of presents in hospital. They are jealous of the extra fuss for the sick child, the family seems to revolve around hospital visits, special treatments and medicines and the other factors of illness. It all seems too much and the feeling that 'mum does not love me as much' can be created without really trying.

There may be considerable resentment that the sick child prevents the normal family way of life and takes most of the spare money and time. They may protest at being left with other people while the sick child has the parents, and seek attention in various ways. The well children may certainly miss out on a normal childhood.

In some areas there are sibling support groups attached to hospital wards or clinics. Not all children benefit from group work, some need individual help, but a group can offer a safe place to talk about feelings and problems. It is usually helpful if an experienced child care nurse can teach the children the basic facts of the illness – what it is, the treatment, any special equipment needed, what it is like to have the illness and to answer other queries.

There should be times for sharing with each other what it is like to live with a sick brother or sister.

Death of a Sibling

When a child in a family dies the feelings of the siblings will be just as important but different from those of the parents and other adults. If the child had a long illness there may be considerable relief – no more hospital visits, special equipment or medication, or being left with friends while mother spends so much time at hospital. The hope would be for life to return to normal, but it cannot. The parents need to struggle with their own grief and are not the way they were to each other or the children.

It would be important to think what the dead child meant to the remaining siblings:

- Were they older or younger than the brother or sister? Is there a large age gap, or is there now only one child?
- Was the child a twin?
- What is missing now? A big brother who used to help with the

computer games, a little sister who wanted stories to be read to her every night, a companion for walks with the dog or cycle rides, someone who argued or teased?

Parents may benefit from some help with addressing the children's needs as their own feelings may be overwhelming. It is common for bereaved parents to idolise the dead child. They may fill the house with pictures, or even keep the bedroom untouched. But, what does that do to the remaining child? It is likely to be confusing – why is the bedroom being left if it is not needed? Perhaps the child is not dead after all. Why is there all this fuss over someone who is not even here? The child may need help to understand the parents' feelings; the parents will need to understand what they could do, unintentionally, to the survivor(s).

Survivor Guilt

The remaining child(ren) can think that the family must have loved the dead child more than them since there are more pictures of that one – 'I should have been the one to die as I was not the favourite'. There may also be considerable guilt that perhaps the death was in some way their fault, and a feeling of being blamed for it.

Guilt may weigh heavily on survivors from a disaster such as a school trip accident or other event when some people suffered. It is usually helpful to allow a debriefing; to go over the event again to be reassured it was not their responsibility.

Death in a School

The death of a school child has a deep effect on the child's class, particularly the close friends, the teachers and the whole school in some way. The teachers have a vital role in supporting the children as they are already known to them and also share the loss.

The death may have happened at school and been witnessed by some children so a careful explanation of the facts will be necessary. A teenager collapsed while playing football and the teacher was desperate to know the reason, fearing that one of the players had attacked him and he had not noticed. The information from the hospital confirming the child had suffered a massive spontaneous brain haemorrhage was a tremendous shock but also a relief as no one was responsible.

The first few days in school after the bad news has been told is when the shock gives way to reality. The children may want to do something. At first they may want to put flowers at the scene of the accident or at the family home. Adults may think this rather morbid or fear it may turn into a shrine, but for the children perhaps it is all they can do. Later on they may go to the funeral, write letters or make pictures for the parents. The class teacher could discuss with the children what they would like as a memorial. Suggestions might include planting a tree in the school garden, a seat in the playground, a special picture or piece of equipment. Some classes have made a memory book to which the children contribute drawings, writings and poems. It is often a good idea for the children to write down their own personal memories to keep.

The school staff may need considerable help especially if none have experienced the death of a student before. Staff meetings may provide a supportive group; it could be helpful to ask a bereavement counsellor to facilitate the group and offer suggestions to help the children. A group for parents may help them support their children.

The children should not be expected to 'be over it' by the end of term, some may need help for a year or more. Some schools offer a quiet room, sessions with the school nurse or year tutor and regular meetings with the parents.

The Changing Needs of the Bereaved Child

Children's concept of time changes with age and so does their understanding since the loss. They have a continuing need to make sense of what has happened, which may mean a regular review of the facts. As their thinking develops, this brings new information needs and new fears. Parents and carers should understand that it is normal rather than an unhealthy curiosity.

For the child who has received a transplanted organ, the need to review the information is similar. The teenager who had a liver transplant several years ago has new questions now – 'Why couldn't my old one be fixed, why did I have to have someone else's?'

When parents separate or divorce and the children live with one parent, they often want to know more about the other parent at some later stage. Teenagers and young adults adopted as young children often have a real need to find information about their natural parents. It was after drinking heavily at a party that Gary, aged 21, decided to find his real father. He had not realised until afterwards how much he had needed to meet him.

Teenagers who have been abused, emotionally, physically or sexually, when younger, will be asking more questions as their knowledge and understanding of what really happened grows. The anger and guilt become stronger, so it is important for these young people to be supported as they begin to face the world as adults. Drugs or alcohol may be tried as an escape from the real world, and eating disorders or self-harm as cries for help.

> There are, thus, many stress to be faced by the child who loses someone with whom he has strong bonds of attachment . . . Yet with the sensitive support of parent or parents will master this trauma. His life and development within the family will go on (Raphael, 1984).

Anniversaries

A year has many days which have special memories for individuals, linked to particular events or people. For a bereaved child these bring added thoughts:

- Christmas is meant to be a happy family time, but someone is missing; last year was such fun – or sad or in a different house. A special decoration could be hung on the tree or a candle lit for the absent person.
- The new year may bring relief that a bad year is over but it may be hard to let go of a year when a major event occurred.
- Birthdays are occasions to remember a person and families and friends can share their thoughts. Children may still like to make a card for the missing person.
- Children may be affected by how the family cope with special days.
- Other important annual occasions might include holidays and visits, also dates of an accident, illness, operations or bad news.

Helping Children with their Feelings

Children have strong feelings, especially anger, guilt and fear, and often the adults in a family are unable to allow a child to express them as they are struggling with their own. They may 'test out' other people – the six-year-old who told everyone in the village 'my brother's dead you know'. A five-year-old who told the teacher quietly 'my mummy's sad because her daddy has died, it was alright because he didn't hurt.'

Sometimes all you can do is acknowledge what is happening and how the child could be feeling: 'Perhaps this is just too terrible to talk about' and 'I expect you are blaming yourself for this'.

Anger may come out after a while: 'Why did this have to happen to me, our family, my school?'

> Ben was 13 when his brother was knocked over and killed on the estate where they lived. He was angry that drivers did not slow down, and great effort went into a house-to-house petition for increased road safety. Discussing the angry feelings and learning ways of managing them included hitting a cushion when he was 'bursting'. A classmate's father had died during the year and the two found they could share similar thoughts. One teacher in particular was very approachable and offered a quiet room for when the child needed to 'opt out' for a short break in the school day.

Traumatic Bereavement

Sometimes death happens in traumatic circumstances – mass disaster, violence, murder, fire, drowning, car crash and children may even have been witness. Pynoos' (1992) studies show that children suffer post-traumatic stress disorder as do adults. They may have dreams, intrusive feelings and reminders of the event, sleep disturbances as well as the normally recognised signs of grieving.

Intervention within a few days of the event is essential to minimise long-term problems. Careful interviewing allows the child to describe in minute detail all that was seen, felt, heard, smelt and remembered. This way the details of the trauma are kept with the event. It is important to deal with the trauma before the child can move on to the actual loss. Regular monitoring of the child should prompt help if problems arise.

Children may suffer in a similar way after a traumatic event such as a hurricane or flood. The sound of thunder and strong winds may stir up fearful memories.

Ways of Helping Children

Always be on the lookout for the effects of unresolved grief – sleeping problems, eating disorders, missing school, poor performance, regression and psychosomatic disorders such as headaches, tummy aches, nausea etc., changes in behaviour – unusually withdrawn, aggressive or uncontrollable.

Anyone involved with children might notice these signs. In fact the child may present with a separate problem, such as going to the family doctor with a worsening of eczema causing severe scratching at night, referral to a child psychologist for a behavioural difficulty or being unable to manage school work. Professionals should ask if this child could be reacting to a loss of any kind.

There does seem to be a general shortage of organised help for bereaved children, although in some areas there are wonderful schemes. Perhaps everyone working with children of all ages needs to be more aware of their plight and not be afraid of helping, by allowing them to talk, to listen and to seek experienced help as needed.

> The kind of support offered should ideally be determined by the needs of the bereaved, but realistically it will depend on what resources are available (Hindmarsh, 1993).

> A good example of local helping grew from a few community nurses who worked in three nearby villages. They had nursed some adults who had died around the same time, leaving children. With the

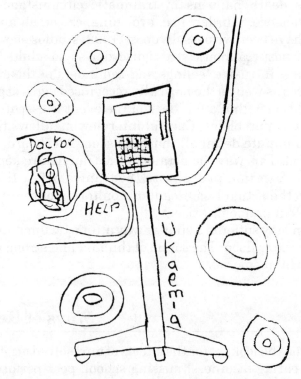

Fig. 6.1 Therapeutic activities for a bereaved children's group could include ways of dealing with anger such as making targets for clay bombs. The boy who drew this was able to express his feelings towards leukaemia and to the doctors who could not make his sibling better.

aim of helping these children, a working party was set up. This involved several professionals with experience – community nurses, a child care nurse, a trained counsellor and a teacher who was also bereavement counsellor. Training, information and resources were shared and a small support group was started for these children. The feedback was positive – the children were able to talk more freely about the dead parent, which helped the lone parent. The children's teachers reported an improvement in school, and the children enjoyed their special group which met fortnightly after school. The parents also met each other and found support themselves by sharing their problems.

There are support groups for bereaved children in many areas, some organised to run regularly, some for a set time or for a particular purpose, such as after a local disaster. Yule and Williams (1990) have studied a group of children who survived the capsize of the ferry Herald of Free Enterprise in Zeebruggge harbour in 1987. Dyregrov (1990) reminds us that 'bereavement groups for children can be very helpful, but adults should be careful that members do not build a new identity around their grief, and be aware that such groups can sometimes be destructive without direction'.

The local branch of CRUSE Bereavement Care may run groups for children or hold holiday playschemes. Some hospitals have groups for siblings of child patients who have died. Some schools offer an after-school group for bereaved children. The several children's hospices around Britain offer continuing care for the family after a death as do many adult hospices. Groups offer a bereaved child a safe place to talk about what has happened and to share feelings with others and with an experienced adult facilitator. Carefully planned play and activities are therapeutic and fun.

Some areas have a Divorce and Consiliation Service which offers counselling for children. Departments of Child Psychiatry and Family Consultation Clinics usually offer family therapy and individual work with children. Skilled use of play is a non-threatening way for a child to relive an event and express feelings. They may refer the child elsewhere for special help, such as after witnessing a parent being murdered.

Resources for the helper include many books and training videos. Branches of CRUSE will often lend them. There is a wide range of books and games for children of all ages. Some of these are available in bookshops, from CRUSE, hospitals, or specialist suppliers.

Financial support for voluntary work may be possible through charity.

Work with bereaved children is not widely known to people outside the field, so it is not surprising that it is not known where to go for help. Start by making enquiries at the health centre, hospital, social services, school, Citizens' Advice Bureau, CRUSE, or any professional involved with children or the incident.

A good local network of those who could offer help, advice and support would be useful so that help is available to all children if they need it.

References

Compassionate Friends (1989) Ideas for parents on how to help children with their grief, prepared by the Compassionate Friends. In *Good Grief (2): Exploring Feelings, Loss and Death*. Good Grief, 19 Bawtree Road, Uxbridge, Middx UB8 1PT. Copyright 1989 Barbara Ward and Associates.

Dyregrov, A. (1990) *Grief in Children – a Handbook for Adults*. London: Jessica Kingsley.

Hindmarsh, C. (1993) *On the Death of a Child*. Oxford: Radcliffe Medical Press.

Le Shan, E. (1976) *Learning to say Goodbye: When a Parent Dies*. New York: Macmillan.

Pynoos, R.S. (1992) Grief and trauma in children and adolescence. *Bereavement Care*, **11(1)**: 2–10.

Raphael, B. (1984) *The Anatomy of Bereavement, a handbook for caring professions*. London: Unwin Hyman.

Wells, R. (1988) *Helping Children Cope with Grief – Facing a Death in the Family*. London: Sheldon Press.

Worden, J.W. (1984) *Grief Counselling and Grief Therapy*, London: Routledge. (2nd edition 1991.)

Yule, W. and Williams, R. (1990) Post-traumatic stress reactions in children. *Journal of Traumatic Stress* **3(2)**: 279–95.

7

Self-Esteem and Loss

Yvonne Gabell

'I feel like I am going to die.' This is how a small boy of eight years describes his feelings when, on a visit, he sees his father's new son climb onto his lap. Clearly this small lad's sense of loss and grief at this moment is so acute that he feels as if he ceases to matter to his father and so might as well not exist.

As you read the above you may have been aware of your feelings. You may have felt a frisson of sympathy, a deep sadness, or a feeling of puzzlement at what might appear to you to be an extreme comment. You may, or may not, be attentive to the usual state of your self-esteem, whether it is 'high' or 'low', of variation in self-esteem and the causes for this. Depending on our upbringing and later experiences, children's grief and loss may well be painful to us, if these remind us of unmourned and perhaps forgotten losses. Conversely, professional carers who are strong, healthy and achievers may find it difficult to understand the lowering of self-esteem in children and underestimate the emotional wear and tear of working with such children. It is necessary to be aware of our own level of self-esteem if we are working with or living among children with low self-esteem.

In this chapter some of the wide range of experiences of grief and loss in children which lead to a lowering of their self-esteem are described. The effects of these are seen in the surgery, ward, classroom and home, where children with a lowered self-esteem generally present at either end of the normal behavioural range, being either very withdrawn or very disruptive. Some general observations on attitudes towards children's self-esteem and creative methods of helping children regain and develop their sense of self-esteem are given in the various sections of the chapter.

Self-Esteem

Although texts on grief and loss in children mention in passing the words 'self-esteem' few discuss what the term means and whether it can be altered or restored. High self-esteem is an appreciation of ourselves and our inherent worth, giving us a sense of our own ability, competence and power and the ability to compare ourselves favourably to others. With low self-esteem we are self-deprecating, helpless, powerless and compare ourselves unfavourably to others (Smelser, 1989).

The general level of a person's self-esteem is formed in early years by the warmth and closeness coming from their primary carer. Some mothers control their growing children by threat of abandonment: 'If you don't behave I'll have you put away!' and 'If you behave like that you'll make me ill!' Unjustified accusations may be made: 'You caused your father's stroke!' Such threats and accusations leave a child anxious and angry and full of guilt. How can they have good self-esteem when so burdened? Families can diminish the self-esteem of children by direct attributions or by overheard remarks: 'She's the plump one' and 'He's like uncle Fred, he never did much'. Bowlby (1988) describes three distinctive patterns of child rearing, each of which leads to a different attitude to the world as the child grows up. Some children form a secure attachment to their mother and grow up as happy children, delightful to have around. These children clearly have a high self-esteem. The second group develop an anxious resistant attachment and tend to be whiny and clinging as they grow up. These children would be less secure and their self-esteem more easily shaken. Thirdly, are those who grow up in the anxious avoidance attitude who tend to keep others at a distance and are prone to bully other children. These might be expected to show low self-esteem as they grow up.

Thus from birth, people grow up with a specific attitude towards themselves and the world. During early childhood this varies dramatically in a short time (Knapp in Bhatti *et al.*, 1989) and is unstable until the age of seven (Martinek and Zaichkowsky, Bhatti *et al.*, 1989). Those with good self-esteem feel generally positive about themselves, other people and situations and face life in all its aspects competently. As part of this competence they acquire social skills, the verbal and non-verbal behaviours which enable people to fit into their society and make positive relationships with others in the various areas of life. Those with low self-esteem feel bad about themselves, other people and situations. They feel they have no control over events, feel incompetent, act so, are seen as incompetent by others, thus fulfilling their expectation! They tend not to acquire positive social skills. They may become socially aggressive which leads to counter-aggression from others and social rejection. In a child this may lead to fighting, bullying, lack of friends and low educational attainment. Alternatively they become passive and withdrawn, unable to express their needs, feelings and ideas. A child will feel inadequate, maybe depressed, which will be shown by anxiety and fear of new situations which hinders learning at school. Children who find it difficult to accept failure, criticism or being ignored may well have low self-esteem.

Loss and Self-Esteem

Positive self-esteem is rooted in the process and product of forming secure attachments:

> Through the process of attachment, the child comes to see him- or herself as a worthwhile, interesting individual who is loveable and who can function in competent, responsible ways in relationship with others and with the world (Jewett, 1994, p. 144).

This process is influenced by the nature and quality of the child's repeated interactions with significant others. The warmth of significant caregivers and the continuity, predictability and dependability of people, relationships and situations provide solid foundations on which secure attachments can be built. Loss threatens and sometimes shatters these foundations and thus undermines self-esteem. When this is compounded by the difficult behaviour, self-blame and feelings of guilt and shame which can accompany loss, a child's self-esteem is massively at risk. The early years of a child's life are especially important in terms of developing secure attachments and self-esteem, but the self-esteem thus acquired is not fixed and is influenced throughout childhood and beyond by the nature and quality of relationships and other experiences. These include the experience of loss.

Children's self-esteem is greatly affected by experiences of loss and grief, especially when losses are many and for those children whose self-esteem is already low. One event in a child's life may lead to multiple loss.

Children whose circumstances deteriorate because of marital breakdown or reduced income associated with a parent's redundancy or ill health are exposed to multiple loss. The child's parents will be 'lost' too; different, sad, angry, depressed. The child will probably move from a familiar area; changing school, losing friends, hobbies, activities and favourite special places. The family may end up in bed and breakfast accommodation, or live temporarily with a series of friends and relations, in which case a child's pet and possessions will probably be lost as well. Unless the situation is explained to the child and space and time given to mourn the losses the child is bound to feel helpless, powerless and of little worth. Similar losses and the same feelings can be experienced by children in care. They are separated from their parents, often from siblings and established friendships, and may have moved around between several children's homes and sets of foster carers because their aggressive or manipulating behaviour is hard to tolerate.

Children who move from one country and culture to another are also subjected to multiple loss. These changes are often so stressful that they trigger further losses such as marital breakdown, and academic failure and under achievement in the child. The comments of a boy going to live in Nigeria with his Nigerian mother, divorced from his English father, pinpoint some of the grief that can come to children born of parents from two cultures or races: 'It's hard enough to know I have to leave my father but it means I have to leave the white part of me also. I feel as if I'm only half a boy now' (Wells, 1988a). The children of refugee families usually experience great uncertainty as well as the actual loss of dispossession. The fate of family members left behind is unknown, their own future is uncertain, and they most likely do not speak the host country's language.

Children's Thinking, Loss and Self-Esteem

Children think differently from adults. Young children experience 'magical thinking' by which they believe that their thoughts make things happen. A child, jealous of the attention shown to a sick sibling may wish this child dead. The sibling dies. The child may be inconsolable, believing he or she directly caused the sibling's death, and through guilt the child loses a sense of self-worth. In a sibling loss survey (Rosen, 1986) 50% of siblings said they felt guilty. They may blame themselves for not helping or refusing to help on one or more occasions when the sibling was sick. They may feel guilty about having a sense of relief at the death, as they think, 'Now people will have time for me!' Sometimes there is anxiety about cause and affect. After the death of a sibling a child may be wondering: 'Did I cause my sister's death?'; 'Could I develop the same disease?'; 'Will I die when I am the same age?'. Only much later, during adolescence, do they eventually progress into the adult stage of 'cognitive thinking' where they develop a sense of values and personal responsibility and are able to assess more accurately the various aspects of a situation.

Unexplained Loss and Self-Esteem

Children's self-esteem can also be threatened by withholding information which could help them understand the losses to which they are exposed. Information may be withheld because adults around them think they are too young to understand or will not notice a change. Unexplained loss can give rise to anxiety, confusion and anger, contributing to negative behaviour patterns and poor relationships which further diminish self-esteem. These problems may not be revealed for some time.

> Heather, aged 13, was referred for counselling by her family, at her school's insistence because of their deep concern at her behaviour. Heather was born and lived in the Middle East until she was two, when the family returned to England. No one thought to explain that, as the move was permanent, Heather would never see her nurse and playmates again. Her mother said that all was well at home, though Heather had not made good peer relationships at primary school, where staff had expressed concern to her parents. Now, in her teens, behavioural problems were acute. Heather argued and caused incidents (stealing money, breaking treasured possessions, hitting people), with her siblings at home and peers at school, always blaming them. She was never in the right place at the right time. Those around Heather were offended and deeply concerned by her wetting and encopresis, for which there was no medical cause. Staff at school had explored all possible school-based options for changing Heather's behaviour, with no positive outcome.
>   The therapist felt that Heather's behaviour was becoming more extreme, and wondered if the key might lie in the issue of the 'right place at the right time'. Counselling times were fixed to enable Heather to miss lessons she disliked! Heather was encouraged to draw as she talked about school, her family and her life story. Her

first drawings were full of violence; then ideal places to live were explored. Some transactional analysis ideas were used to give Heather a sense of choice and control, and she became more willing to 'own' her behaviour. Gradually a great sense of grief and loss become conscious which was seen to be linked to the unexplained loss of her first home. Her grief was expressed and plans made for a future visit to the Middle East. The negative behaviour patterns lessened, relationships improved and led to an increased level of self-esteem. Then a sense of belonging and of being at ease in this country was possible.

Sometimes information is withheld or denied because adults are ashamed. When a parent has committed suicide, children may be told that their parent died of a heart attack even though the children may have been present at the time of the overdose. The children then lose a sense of trust in their own perceptions of events and so of their sense of competence to observe events, thus threatening their self-esteem.

Internal Conflict, Loss and Self-Esteem

Grief involves ambivalence and internal conflict. This makes it difficult for children to sustain positive feelings about themselves, and their often troublesome behaviour makes it difficult for others to give them favourable and encouraging feedback. Unless experiences of grief and loss are interpreted to children and they are helped to recognise and work through their ambivalent feelings towards themselves and others, they are bound to feel helpless and powerless and lacking in worth. How this is manifested depends on the child's age. Young children, aged three to five, lack language developed enough to articulate their feelings and will often regress in their behaviour, demanding to be cuddled all the time or to be spoon fed. Children aged six to eight are often grief stricken and will be tearful or aggressively demanding of attention. From the age of nine to 12 anger may predominate.

Wayne, aged 12, was permanently excluded from school. He was sensitive to the slightest criticism or comment from staff or pupils. Wayne frequently lost his temper, expressing his anger, both verbally and physically, swearing at staff and pupils and throwing things. He was critical of the staff and ambivalent about his own abilities, which were of an average level. Life at secondary school became untenable for Wayne. The counsellor surmised that Wayne's anger was not derived from school-based problems, but from unresolved grief. His mother had died several years earlier after a short illness in hospital. No one told Wayne or his brothers of his mother's death, which occurred one Thursday. The boys were sent to school as usual on Friday. On Sunday an uncle told the boys that their mother had died. The cremation and wake were held on the Tuesday while the boys were at school, unaware of these events. On Thursday, a week since his mother's death, Wayne went to bed for three weeks. Wayne missed sharing the immediate grief and mourning of the adult family and had never been able to discuss the loss with anyone.

Wayne was given individual tuition at home. During his lessons, opportunities were taken to discuss Wayne's opinions and attitudes. It was difficult to interest Wayne in work as 'I hate . . .' was the response. Time was spent exploring the 'I hate' theme and the possible reasons behind it. At the same time a wider and scaled vocabulary of words that could be used to give criticism were introduced and positive 'likes' gradually identified. Wayne's ability to relate positively to others was hindered by simplistic observations, 'all teachers are useless' being one such statement. This was analysed and the more accurate observation of 'some teachers are useless' emerged!

Various outings were arranged to give relaxed spaces where discussion might occur. On one of these visits, to look at the architecture of a church and village, Wayne asked to walk around the churchyard and began to talk about the death of his mother, and his feelings about the family's behaviour at the time of the funeral. Wayne was encouraged to verbalise his grief and anger at his loss and the family's response, and to look forward to regaining a positive attitude to his future life which, it was suggested, was what his mother would have wished for him. Wayne was found a place at a smaller school which he attended with much grief resolved and more positive attitudes towards himself and others.

Bereaved teenagers may act as if nothing has happened, the denial mode, or they may act out their anger in self-destructive behaviour, cutting themselves, stealing and driving fast cars; they may seek means of escape from the pain of grief and loss in solvent, drug, or alcohol abuse, or promiscuity.

Altered Body Image, Loss and Self-Esteem

Adolescents, and increasingly younger children, are much influenced by media images when judging themselves. Eight-year-olds now discuss weight and talk of dieting, anorexia and bulimia. In adolescence, boys' and girls' sense of self-esteem is also influenced very much by the opinions of their peers. They measure their worth by the response of others and that response depends so much on the 'right' appearance. Any child who does not conform to this image whether because of personal attributes or insufficient money to buy the 'right' clothes, or other reasons, may suffer a sense of loss personally and be teased and bullied. A child born with a disability, physical or mental, will not only grow up with the specific loss but also with the parent's grief at their birth. In families with high self-esteem, children with disabilities are accepted with love, understanding and appropriate support. Other families find acceptance much more difficult. There may be blame, guilt and depression among family members.

Children who have a chronic illness and those with physical or mental handicaps can have precarious self-esteem. They see others able to do so many things they cannot and often face isolation both practically and as a result of society's attitudes towards them. Self-esteem is partly dependent on acceptance by society, so lack of acceptance for any reason may lower a child's self-esteem. Parents and carers each have their own ideas, conscious and unconscious, of what is acceptable and pleasant and they need to be aware that these may be passed verbally and non-verbally to the children they are caring for.

The self-esteem of pre-school children with chronic illness or disability can be further undermined by behavioural difficulties exhibited by them. These may be due to spells in hospital, causing them to be separated from their parents at a young age, to periods of enforced inactivity due to the illness, and to anxiety about their future. The difficulties may also be due to either over-lax or over-strict upbringing caused by parental anxiety (Richman, 1988).

For adolescents peer group acceptance is of prime importance. Any disability which makes an adolescent stand out from their friends lowers self-esteem. Acne and other skin disorders may make them feel, or be called, untouchable. Those suffering from diabetes, where the necessary concern for regular eating patterns does not fit into the normal rather chaotic pattern of teenage life, can feel uncomfortable with their peers. Frequent stays in hospital can destroy friendship networks, especially in rural areas where the specialist units may be far distant from the child's home. Hospital routine with its own rules can lead to a loss of the identity and independence so important to adolescents. All these losses undermine an adolescent's self-esteem.

Children with severe learning and physical disabilities who live in residential homes have particular problems in developing a high self-esteem. They rarely see other children to experience the outside world where children are active and allowed to make choices as they grow up. The children they meet, like themselves, have specific problems with movement and communication, so it is difficult to form relationships and learn everyday social skills. Frustration due to difficulty in communicating their needs and wishes often leads to behavioural problems which further inhibit the development of a positive self-esteem.

Children's self-image can be altered suddenly and dramatically by an accident or the onset of malignant disease. The case below illustrates how one such loss was dealt with in a constructive way.

> Tom, aged 15, after developing Crohn's disease, had surgery which left him with a stoma. Tom was fortunate in many ways. His mother accepted the need for the operation and the resulting aftercare in a positive way. Tom's school was also helpful. The Year Head encouraged Tom's friends to visit him in hospital and kept in touch by letter. The school nurse made the necessary arrangements for Tom's care at school for when he would return. Tom's self-esteem remained high in this atmosphere of acceptance and hope. Even so he still had concerns which needed to be addressed:
>
> * How would he cope at school?
> * What would others think?
> * Would he smell?
> * Would he be able to have children?
>
> His adult friends 'heard' these worries and addressed them by inviting several adults and young people who had had a similar operation to visit Tom so that he could learn ways of coping by discussing his situation with those who had already faced, and were living with, a similar loss of body function and altered self-image.

Children who develop cancer may suffer hair loss as part of the treatment, and feel very scared at the prospect of a return to school. This can lead to a loss of self-esteem, and thought needs to be given to how to deal with this. A cheerful resolution at one primary school was that all the boys were allowed to wear baseball caps, indoors as well as out, until their friend's hair regrew. Adams-Greenly (1984) identified the promotion of self-esteem through mastery as one of seven principles of helping children communicate about serious illness and death. She describes how a seven-year-old boy with cancer talked with his classmates about the recent amputation of his left arm, as a way of mastering his trauma and so promote his self-esteem. This child was helped by his teacher who reinforced his positive feelings about his experience, helped him answer some of his classmates' questions and developed a teaching plan about cancer and how handicapped people can live normal lives. Ross and Ross (1984) describe a training programme for teaching children with leukaemia to handle ridicule about their altered body image in the form of teasing by peers, and the beneficial effects of this programme on children's self-confidence.

With improved medical treatment, children with chronic conditions spend less time in hospital and more at home. This would appear to be good for the sick child's self-esteem but may be a greater strain for the siblings who daily see the sick child taking so much time and attention away from them (S. Crowley, personal communication 1995). Siblings can feel resentful at being neglected and then guilty about these feelings and become self-critical and lacking in self-esteem. It is helpful for friends or relations to be aware of this and make arrangements, perhaps offering to have the sick child regularly for a few hours or longer, so that parents can have special time for their other children.

A new concern may be arising for disabled children. There is widespread discussion about and use of abortion as a birth control for foetuses which may have a congenital abnormality, and increasing discussion of euthanasia. What effect does such discussion have on a disabled or seriously ill child? What will that child feel? What is society saying about the child's value?

The emergence of 'self-advocacy' groups, for example 'People First' which began in Canada and now has groups in England, represents an important development. It is important that disabled children and their carers are informed of these groups and put in touch with them so that, hopefully, they will have more say in the planning of their future life which will certainly improve their self-esteem.

Grief and Loss in the Family and Self-Esteem

After a death in the family, children experience the feelings usually associated with grief. Bewildering thoughts, questions and feelings are likely to undermine the child's sense of competence, leading to anxiety and a lowering of self-esteem. Aggression may be expressed at school or in the home and dealt with inappropriately. Feelings of isolation and abandonment also undermine self-esteem. Children may feel exhausted and be unable to concentrate on school work, especially difficult for adolescents with examinations to tackle. For them special arrangements can be made and the examining board informed. For children who have lost a parent before they were ten years old, 'A greater tendency to low self-esteem, depression and nervous breakdown have all been cited as persisting effects' (Marshall, 1992, p. 71). When a death has followed a period of illness the effect on children's self-esteem is likely to be less devastating if they have been allowed to share, appropriately, in the nursing and care for their parent or sibling (Brown, 1980). After a death, a friend or relation recognising a child is in distress, can help maintain or develop the child's esteem by asking questions to enable the child to express concerns: 'What do you think will be different now?'. The child can be helped by having the normality of feelings of anger and despair affirmed as well as the need for mourning. The time mourning takes can be explained and the pain to be faced on anniversaries of special events can be talked about. To have someone listen attentively while the child talks about all the events that have happened, and about the person who has died, is a great gift for that child: 'For trauma is bad – being unable to express it is worse' (Miller, 1988, p. 257).

Divorce is another family event that undermines a child's self-esteem. The ongoing California Children of Divorce Study (Whitehead, 1994) supports this, finding that five years after the breakdown of a marriage, one-third of the children suffered from moderate to severe depression and ten years after, a significant number were rootless and under-achieving. After divorce (or a parent's death) remarriage may follow long before that time has elapsed and the anger at the loss of the birth parent may be transferred to the new step-parent. Wells observes that a child can mourn for three to five years after the child's parents have separated and that 'a stepfamily is a family born of loss' (Wells, 1993, p. 81).

Loss in Education and Self-Esteem

Life itself in a school is a cause of grief for some pupils, especially for those who enter the educational system with low self-esteem. Each school has its own ethos. Any child who does not fit in whether by health, physical appearance, clothes, speech, class, address, or family circumstances may feel lost or left out, and react to this feeling.

If the child has grown up with a good self-esteem and carers with whom the child can talk, problems will be surmounted and temporary drops in self-esteem survived. But other children do not find life so easy. They may respond in a variety of ways, by bullying or be so withdrawn that they are bullied. Bullying poses a tremendous threat to a child's self-esteem. A questionnaire on bullying in schools in Sheffield (Muisener, 1994) reported that 27% of junior/middle school children and 10% of secondary school children were being bullied. The bullies, the victims and those who are both bully and victims (who bully the very weak and are victimised by the strong) are children suffering from low self-esteem. If bullying goes un-noticed or is ignored, the victim may under-achieve or become a school refuser or truant and, in extreme cases, even commit suicide. A firm school policy towards bullying can reduce its incidence, but a few will continue to bully as a way of bolstering their self-esteem unless they receive help. Assertiveness training and counselling to discuss the reasons for their unhappiness can greatly help.

Pupils who become aggressive to staff, refuse to study, become unable to study or become the class clown, may well be feeling sadness, having suffered some unacknowledged or unmourned loss, or may have grown up with a low self-esteem. Time needs to be spent with them at home or school to explore their experiences and feelings.

Staff need to be aware of pupils whose parents are disabled, ill or dying and take appropriate steps to monitor their progress and needs.

> Nick was truanting from secondary school for no apparent reason. A brief counselling session elicited the fact that Nick liked school, was liked and had been doing well, but his father had died several years before, and his mother was now seriously ill. Nick was scared to leave her in case he returned to find her dead. It was agreed that Nick would go home each lunchtime to see his mother. These brief midday visits enabled Nick to resettle in school.

Some losses are not so apparent. The academic 'low achiever' in a highly academic family, though of average intelligence, can feel under-valued and useless at home. At school they may be teased in class for 'crawling' when working hard to please the family. These children may benefit from a simple explanation of the intelligence spread across the population and some discussion of what makes for happiness and contentment. With self-esteem restored they can go on to achieve positively for their own self-satisfaction. The opposite situation is also difficult. The bright child in a family who regard academic success fearfully, possibly because of their bad experience at school, may be discouraged from achieving because the family feel the child will grow away from them. These children may feel powerless, and out of step with their family and friends. They need as much understanding and encouragement as the less able child, especially around the age of 16 when decisions must be made concerning college or university studies which their family may well be strongly discouraging. It will be difficult for them to make a free choice.

The Children Act (Department of Health, 1989) entitles children with Special Educational Needs, whether academic, social or physical, to extra support in school. The amount received varies. Some of these children have very low self-esteem, expressing a feeling of helplessness and even despair, which is not helped by their peers, or sadly sometimes adults, who may refer to them as the 'thickies' if they are academically behind for their age. Children still use words such as 'spastic' as a term of abuse in conversation, which is painful for a child suffering any physical disability. By listening carefully to children's perceptions of themselves, often expressed in throwaway remarks such as 'I'm stupid' in the middle of a sentence about work, or even complaining that they are not working because it is too easy, it is possible to perceive and address the low self-esteem of that child. It may help to discuss what makes a person valuable. In recent years there has been a move to integrate children with a physical disability into mainstream schools, believing that this will increase their self-esteem. In many cases this has been achieved, maybe with the help and support of a welfare assistant, but not always. A child's level of self-esteem needs constant monitoring if the child is placed in a situation where their abilities are very different from those around them, and work needs to be done with the peer group so that they understand the needs and potential of the child who has the disability.

Loss in Society and Self-Esteem

Children who do not fulfil society's expectations of their behaviour in loss and grief may experience guilt, both their own and that given them by others. Children may be told to 'be good' because their parents are upset. Older ones may be expected to give up their future plans to look after the surviving parent.

Children express their grief differently from adults. A small child of four, on being told of the death of his mother, may ask after a few moments if he can go out to play. Death as a reality has no meaning for him. Older children may mourn intensely for short periods which recur, this pattern of intermittent intense mourning can extend in time longer than an adult might expect (Wells, 1988). Those around may presume the child has 'got over it'. Children may grieve for those whom grown-ups do not expect them to. Abrams (1992) writes movingly of her grief at the loss of her stepfather, something which those around did not understand, leaving her feeling misunderstood.

Many adults as well as children are scared of grief and keep away from those who mourn, so leading to feelings of isolation. A girl aged 16, whose father had died some months earlier, noted how friends and neighbours crossed the street to avoid her mother and herself when they were out shopping. Friends at school, not knowing what to say, may avoid the bereaved child at playtimes and not call round to play after school. It is supportive if a child can be told of and perhaps introduced to another child who has suffered a similar loss. Children are sometimes stigmatised by society. Children have been refused play-group and school places because they or their siblings are HIV positive or have AIDS. Such attitudes lead to a need for secrecy in families which separates children from their friends and makes them feel different, a cause for low self-esteem, as all children wish to be as like their friends as possible. Similarly children with parents in prison often suffer not only from the loss of that parent, sometimes for many years, but also from other children's avoidance of them.

Suicide, Loss and Self-Esteem

Suicide is the most extreme expression of lack of self-esteem and may be attempted, sometimes successfully, for reasons, such as disappointing examination results or broken friendships, that others regard as trivial. Any threat or hint of suicide must be taken seriously and openly discussed with the child. The discussion itself can lower the risk, as the child comes to share fears and despairs and realises, perhaps for the first time, that such problems and feelings are not unique. Knowledge that members of the Samaritan organisation and various 'helplines' are there to listen when grief seems overwhelming can be helpful to a child who feels of little or no worth. If there is doubt about the child's state of mind, clearly the child will need to be encouraged to seek medical help. Sometimes the threat occurs because of a breakdown in family communication. In these circumstances family therapy can encourage more positive sharing of feelings, a reframing of problems and show alternative ways of resolving conflicts.

Regaining and Developing Self-Esteem

Throughout this chapter suggestions have been made as to how children can be helped to regain and develop their self-esteem with regard to specific situations, although most can also be applied generally.

There are many creative ways of enabling children to face the prospect and actuality of grief and loss, and to express and acknowledge their feelings. They can, as appropriate for their age and ability, express feelings in clay or paint. Drama and role play can be used to help children of any age express and work through grief and anger. Older children can be encouraged to write poetry or to keep a journal. Children in care are often helped to draw a lifeline to reduce confusion caused by moves and changes of carer, or to make an ongoing scrap book, including photos and letters to affirm the positive in their lives. For children whose parents are terminally ill, it is helpful to enable them to write or draw their 'goodbyes' before the parent dies (Black, 1989).

Some children wish to speak about their grief or loss and are able to do so, receiving understanding, support and help appropriately. Others, who are clearly showing signs of a loss of self-esteem, may be unable, or find it difficult to tell their story. There are 'ways in' to enable children to explore their story, and for their carers to acknowledge and accompany them in their grieving.

- *Shields*. Children from the age of ten years can be given an outline shield (Fig. 7.1) to complete. During, or after the completion, the various responses can be explored by discreet questioning or comment. Figure. 7.2 was drawn by an 11-year-old boy whose mother had left the family, leaving three children with their father. The boy's shield shows his fears about the transfer to secondary school, (three months earlier). He discussed the 'losing friends' comment and the rather sad epitaph, 'he always wanted a happy life' which suggested that he was not expecting to have one.
- *A Family Drawing*. A girl of 11 was referred for counselling because in her first term of secondary school she was frequently in tears and suffering acute headaches, especially when corrected. Medical advice was sought about the headaches. The detail of her drawing (Fig. 7.3) showed a need to be perfect in lessons, the resulting loss of self-esteem being shown by tears when corrected. 'NAN' written in capital letters, compared to other family members written in small case was significant; Nan had died several months earlier. 'Myself' at the end of and rather apart from the family line, showed that she was missing her mother acutely. At primary school she had seen her mother, a helper there, regularly during the day. A week after the drawing

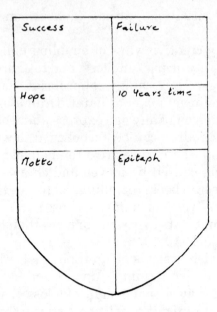

Fig. 7.1 Outline shield.

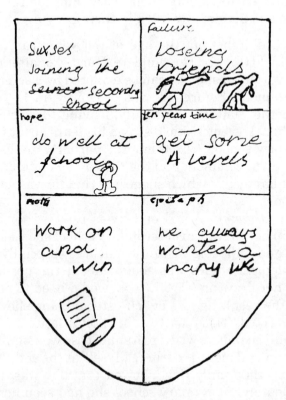

Fig. 7.2 Completed shield, boy aged 11.

Dad MuM. NAN Sister MYSELF

Fig. 7.3 Family drawing, girl aged 11.

 session, she managed a couple of days at school without tears. Not all children draw as well as the example shown in Fig. 7.3, and 'stick' families can be useful for exploring family grief and loss.

- *Drawing a Tree.* This can be a useful activity for children age eight and above. Children with good self-esteem draw trees which are rooted, have a strong trunk and a good crown of branches and/or leaves. Some children add fruit and have nests for birds and holes for small animals or woodpeckers (Fig 7.4 and 7.5). The other drawings of a tree (Figs 7.6 and 7.7) are strikingly different. It would need sensitive questioning about the missing crown to encourage these children to share, if they wished, the losses in their lives.

- *Genograms.* Adolescents can be asked to draw a special family tree, the genogram. Detailed family information is revealed without difficult questioning. Discretion is needed in the amount of comment made and interpretation given to the child. Figure 7.8 shows the genogram of an 18-year-old girl, Mary. There was concern because she was depressed and angry with those around her. Her family was close knit. Mary had had two major operations recently. Her godmother, a cousin aged 29, was seriously ill when the genogram was drawn, and died soon after. Analysis of the genogram shows a great many untimely deaths in the

Fig. 7.4 Tree, girl aged 11.

family, some of which had 'age echoes'. There were many marriage separations.

A child who is suffering a loss of self-esteem through grief or loss is not helped by the helping adults around them becoming angry or overly sympathetic. Children have strengths and it is more creative to focus on these when looking to the future than to speak and act

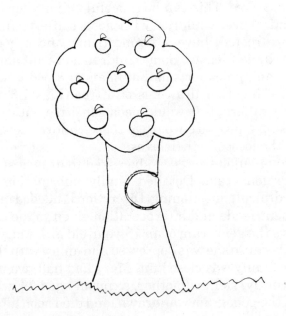

Fig. 7.5 Tree, girl aged 11.

Fig. 7.6 Tree, boy aged 11.

as if despair will continue for ever. White (1988) in his work with individuals and families, focuses on specific types of focused questioning to enable those who have experienced grief and loss to

Fig. 7.7 Tree, boy aged 11.

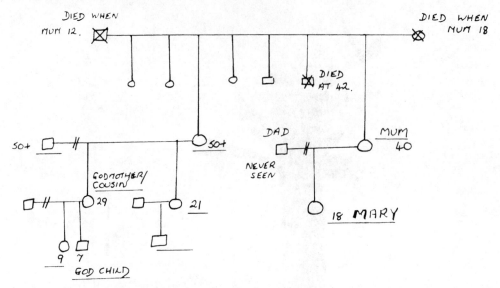

Fig. 7.8 Genogram, girl aged 18. (□, male; ○, female; ×, died; //, divorced; —, live same road.)

discover the 'unique outcome', believing that each person can find a constructive way to cope with their grief and loss and then go on to live a fulfilling life.

Conclusion

This chapter has explored ways in which the grief and loss experienced by children may lead to a loss in self-esteem, and has shown that the extent of such loss depends on many factors. Children who have been brought up with a good level of self-esteem and are allowed time and space to mourn their loss and given loving support will regain their usual good level of self-esteem in due course. For others the grief and loss may lead to a more traumatic loss of self-esteem, especially if they have had little chance to develop good self-esteem. These children will need more time, space and loving support from those around them, and may be helped to regain and develop their sense of self-esteem by the use of some of the ideas and techniques outlined in this chapter.

References

Adams-Greenly, M. (1984) Helping children communicate about serious illness and death. *Journal of Psychosocial Oncology*, **2**: 61.

Abrams, R. (1992) *When Parents Die*. London: Letts.

Bhatti, B., Derezotes, D., Seung-Ock, K. and Specht, H. (1989) The association between child maltreatment and self-esteem. In A.M. Mecca, N.J. Smelser, and J. Vasconcellos (Eds), *The Social Importance of Self-Esteem*. London: University of California Press.

Black, D. (1989) Family therapy and life threatening illness in children and parents. *Palliative Medicine*, **3**: 113.

Bowlby, J. (1988) *A Secure Base. Clinical Applications of Attachment Theory*. London: Routledge.

Brown, F.H. (1989) The impact of death and serious illness on the family life cycle. In E.A. Carter and M. McGoldrick (Eds), *The Changing Family Life Cycle*. London: Allyn and Bacon.

Department of Health (1989) *The Children Act 1989*. London: HMSO.

Jewett, C. (1994) *Helping Children Cope with Separation And Loss*. London: Batsford.

Marshall, F. (1992) *Losing a Parent*. London: Sheldon Press.

Miller, A. (1988) *For Your Own Good. The Roots Of Violence in Child Rearing*. London: Virago Press.

Muisener, P.P. (1994) *Understanding and Treating Adolescent Substance Abuse*. London: Sage.

Richman, N. (1988) Overview of Behaviour and Emotional Problems. In: Richman, N. and Lansdown, R. (Eds), *Problems of Pre-School Children*. Chichester: Wiley.

Rosen, H. (1986) *Unspoken Grief, Coping With Childhood Sibling Loss*. Massachusetts: Lexington Books.

Ross, D.M. and Ross, S.A. (1984) Teaching the Child with Leukemia to Cope with Teasing. *Issues in Comprehensive Pediatric Nursing* **7**: 59.

Smelser, N.J. (1989) Self-Esteem and Social Problems: An Introduction. In: A.M. Mecca, N.J. Smelser, and J. Vasconcellos (Eds), *The Social Importance of Self-Esteem*, London: University of California Press.

Wells, R. (1988) *Helping Children Cope with Grief*. London: Sheldon Press.

Wells, R. (1993) *Helping Children Cope with Divorce*. London: Sheldon Press.

White, M. (1988) Saying Hello Again: The Incorporation of the Lost Realtionship in the Resolution of Grief. *The Dulwich Centre Newsletter*, The Dulwich Centre, Adelaide, South Australia, Spring.

Whitehead, B.D. (1994) Divorce and Kids. The Evidence is In. *Readers Digest* July.

8
Situations of Violence, Abuse and Neglect

Marian Brandon

There has been considerable emphasis in recent years on the need for health professionals to work with colleagues in other professions, particularly social services, in identifying child abuse. There has been much less attention paid to the contact which health workers have in the course of their daily duties with children who have experienced abuse and separation. It is essential for all professionals working with children to be aware of the impact of abuse and loss on all aspects of a child's development and relationships. This awareness needs then to be built into models of good practice which allow health professionals to play their part in contributing to meeting the needs of children.

This chapter will provide a discussion of the meaning of loss for children who have experienced violence or abuse. The impact of maltreatment from parents, is considered and from others outside the family, where the effects on the child may be different. Chapter 9 considers the consequences for children when the abuse, and the circumstances surrounding it, is so serious that children need to be separated from their family and placed in foster or residential care. The work of nursing professionals with children at each stage will be examined.

The Impact of Abuse

Understanding of what constitutes child abuse, maltreatment or, in the words of the Children Act 1989, 'significant harm' to a child, will vary over time. It will also be dependent on the dominant social attitude toward what is, and is not, acceptable behaviour by adults, usually parents, who are responsible for the care and well being of children.

Although the legislation and procedural guidance concerning child protection focuses very much on harm from parents, there is also a warning that professionals intervening should not cause harm to the child by their actions. Furniss (1991) has spoken of secondary damage and traumatisation which can result from an unco-ordinated professional response. The inter-agency guide *Working Together* warns that care needs to be taken in determining whether or not to intervene at all:

> The balance needs to be struck between taking action designed to protect the child from abuse whilst at the same time protecting him or her and the family from the harm caused by the unnecessary intervention (Department of Health, 1991, p.27).

Working Together acknowledges that skills in this area of work are crucial to the immediate and long-term safety and well being of the child. It is in the area of 'well being' that health professionals may have most to contribute. Once abuse is suspected, and a referral made, immediate protection of the child usually falls to social services as key investigator in the case. Child death inquiries have, however, stressed the importance of shared responsibility between agencies at all stages and this is spelled out in *Working Together*. Health professionals, have an important role to play both at this early stage, and later when the investigative flurry has died down and the longer-term implications of abuse and separation need to be considered.

Although not always regarded as key actors in child protection, health professionals are well placed to provide the kind of supportive help to the child and family that has been found to be so important in outcome studies (Farmer and Owen, 1995; Thoburn *et al.*, 1995). This is reiterated in the Audit Commission (1994) report which talks of an overemphasis on investigation, which can in some cases be at the expense of helping the abused child and supporting the family.

What must not be forgotten, however, is the risk to health posed by abuse in childhood:

> Longitudinal studies especially in the field of psychiatry, have underlined the need to protect children by suggesting that abuse in childhood is to be regarded as a risk factor every bit as dangerous as serious childhood illness (Cleaver and Freeman, 1995).

Determining Significant Harm

The wording of 'significant harm' in the Children Act 1989 has required a shift in practice away from determining what abuse is, to ascertaining the *effect* of maltreatment or neglect on the child.

The harm to the child might be of a broader nature than the mere actions or lack of action (for example neglect) of the parent(s). Using definitions of impairment of health or development in the Children Act, it is easier to determine where the harm to a particular child is coming from and then manifesting itself, rather than looking solely to the action of the abuser, and categorising the harm from the abuse that way, to understand the detriment to the child. The site of the damage and consequent losses to the child may thus be located in the following areas, in many combinations:

- ill – treatment (physical, or sexual or emotional);
- impairment of health (physical, mental, emotional);
- impairment of development (physical, intellectual, emotional, social and behavioural).

The effects of the harm might be different for different children, and it is important to remember the *likely* harm to the child in the future, which might not be apparent at this stage. Having provided a broad overview of the harms a child might suffer, it is important to bear in mind the particular losses a child who has been abused might face. This will be examined in detail through case studies demonstrating the losses for children in the early stages of abuse, when they are most likely to remain at home.

Long- and Short-term Consequences of Violence, Abuse and Neglect in Terms of the Losses Experienced

It would be wrong to assume that any one type of abuse (be it sexual, emotional, physical injury or neglect) is of itself more harmful than any other. The severity of the abuse is obviously significant, but the single assault that is harmful and indeed traumatic to one child may be far less damaging to another child. Many children suffer more than one type of maltreatment or neglect and it is the cumulative effect of this and the context of the harm that can create long-term damage.

The context of family life and parenting is also important to a child's health and well-being. Parenting that is 'low on warmth and high on criticism' is known to be harmful (Thoburn *et al.*, 1995). The capacity of parents to provide this warmth is put under threat by stressors such as poverty, unemployment and lack of a supportive relationship from an adult. The damaging effect of long-term family violence is becoming recognised. Children who regularly see their mother beaten can suffer as much as if they had been frequently and severely beaten themselves. Children living in an atmosphere of domestic violence who are also abused or neglected are doubly victimised.

The importance of the context of abuse is reinforced by a Dutch study of the long-term consequences of sexual abuse (Draijer, 1994). A long list of problems found in this random study of 1054 women in the population of the Netherlands, included depression, anxiety, mistrust, problems in relationships, suicidal ideation, eating disorders, agoraphobia, sexual disorders and so on. Thirty-three percent of these women had experienced sexual abuse (Draijer, 1994).

In connecting abuse with the disorders, this study found, however, that the *context* in which the abuse took place was more important in determining later psychopathology, than the *nature* of the abuse itself. Major findings were that a lack of maternal warmth and neglect were more important than the occurrence of sexual abuse itself in suggesting long-term difficulties.

What this means for the child is an accumulation of loss and deficits; loss or lack of the emotional availability of a prime carer, and a lack of basic comfort gained through having basic needs met, which was compounded by sexual abuse. The sexual abuse itself could rarely be seen as the major or sole cause of later problems.

The child's capacity to recover from sexual and other abuse is closely connected with the prime carer's ability to provide a loving and supportive environment for the child. This has been confirmed in a recent UK study of professional intervention in this area (Jones *et al.*, in preparation). The Draijer study found that sexual abuse was more detrimental in the long-term than physical abuse, but suicidality was strongly predicted by a combination of physical and sexual abuse. As a single type of maltreatment, sexual abuse is more predictive of later psychopathology than other abuses, but the greatest risk to later difficulties for all was posed by early separation from a mother or mother figure. So separation in itself is potentially highly damaging: when it is compounded with abuse the child suffers a double blow.

Severity of Consequences of Sexual Abuse

Severity factors are:

- the age of the child (the younger the child the worse the consequences);
- secrecy;
- abuse from a parent.

If sexual abuse is combined with another abuse the effects can be much worse.

The effects of the resilience of the individual child are still largely unknown, but studies on temperament (Rutter and others) suggest that the difficult, hard to settle baby who startles easily may be prone to difficulties through life. A 'hard to parent' child, and this includes children with disabilities, compounds the everyday stresses experienced by parents, and may be more likely to be abused by parents.

The Meaning of Grief and Trauma in the Context of Abuse

Every abused child is in some way victimised, but not every abused child is traumatised. Working with children who have been traumatised requires an understanding of the potential impact on the developing child. These abusive influences will effect how a child develops and grows.

One manifestation of a trauma response is post-traumatic stress disorder (American Psychiatric Association, 1987). In brief this appears in three major clusters:

- as a recurring, intrusive memory which can be in the form of flashbacks to the abusive event, or in recurring bad dreams;
- as a persistent avoidance of stimuli, which can produce a brain-numbing effect, a sense of being cut off or detached or having a reduced involvement in their own world;
- as persistent increased arousal, which may be a state of constant readiness for fight or flight, or a persistent state of fear.

These effects can overwhelm the coping responses of the child. They are defined by behaviour, and by the child's cognitive and physiological responses. They also affect the development of the brain:

> the brain develops and organises as a reflection of developmental experience, so that fear, threat, unpredictability, pain, chaos and hunger can form the template of the brain's fight or flight response (Boat, 1994).

The lingering fear state can be reactivated by each abusive event producing maladaptive behaviours. These behaviours might be:

- oppositional, defiant behaviour;
- a sensitised fear response;
- dissociation, a flight reaction;
- resistant and aggressive behaviours, possibly with the child behaving like a cornered wild animal.

(These behaviours have much in common with the list drawn up by Mrazek and Mrazek (1985) of the short-term effects of physical abuse namely: anhedonia, poor social interaction, poor self-esteem, withdrawal, oppositionality, hypervigilence and pseudo adult behaviour.)

There are two levels of severity of trauma with different characteristics. The first type would involve a single blow or a single event. The trauma associated with this may include a full detailed memory of what occurred, perhaps with the child's own explanations as to why it happened.

The second type concerns long-standing situations of abuse or maltreatment in which patterns of behaviour and coping may develop. In these circumstances there may be a sense of denial or numbing, which can then become a state of self-hypnosis and dissociation, perhaps as a preparation of the body for the abuse which is to come, so the child may create a 'day-time self' and a 'nighttime self'. Then may come rage which can be directed outwards to others, or inwards to the self as self-harm.

These patterns are evident not only in children who have been physically or sexually abused, but may occur in children who regularly witness domestic violence (NCH, 1994). Professionals working with these children may not be alert to this possibility and misunderstand their difficult behaviour. Health professionals, particularly those providing a universal service, can advise parents of the harmful effects of their behaviour on children. They can also provide time and space for a child to talk about these worries.

Health Professionals' Early Contacts with Children who are under Investigation for Harm

Case 1

> Aaron is two and a half. He has a baby sister of five months. His parents are 20 years old and have a violent, stormy relationship. His father has a criminal record including offences of violence, but not against children. His mother says that Aaron is just like his father and has his father's foul temper. She says he is a difficult child to look after, impossible to please, not like his little sister who's good as gold and always asleep.

Aaron was admitted to hospital because of a neighbour's report that she had seen Aaron's mother throw him across a room. He had bruising to his head, his leg and his foot. He was detained in hospital with his parents' consent for 24 hours for observation. His mother went with him.

The ward nurses fulfilled an important role at this stage. There were several elements that could help to identify the likelihood of this child suffering harm currently, or in the future. These include the following.

- *Medical checks to provide evidence of new or old injuries and evidence of development (physical, social and emotional).* The injuries were recorded and charted by the registrar who examined the child, and were used in the subsequent child protection conference.
- *Observation of the child.* This was done by ward nurses and gave a richness to the physical checks undertaken above and helped in the interpretation of harm or likely harm at the conference. How did he look? Did he appear physically well cared for? Did his physical appearance give an indication of his health and development (small or tall, heavy or light for his age in comparison with the size of his parents)? Did his demeanour and behaviour give an indication of his emotional development and

well being? Did he appear traumatised? Did he look alert and interested, did he avoid eye contact, did he exhibit any signs of 'frozen watchfulness', was he sullen and anxious, was he over-friendly with ward staff and indiscriminately seeking or offering affection? In general, how did his behaviour and demeanour compare with other children of his age in a hospital setting?

- *Listening to the child*. With a child as young as Aaron, 'listening' will include hearing any words or phrases he might say, but also looking for other non-verbal ways that he is communicating comfort or discomfort, happiness or stress or distress. Even with older, more verbal children, listening will involve attending to non-verbal cues as well.

- *Observation of relationships*. What was his relationship with his mother like? Was his relationship with his father or other important adults different; how do they compare? (Because Aaron's father was absent this could not be observed, but his mother could be asked how he got on with his father. In this case she said he was a daddy's boy and got on well with his father.) Did he cling to parents? Once settled, did he play but return to his mother for reassurance occasionally? (Aaron was very friendly to all staff and discriminated little between them and his mother; this was a cause for concern.)

- *Observation of the parents*. How did Aaron's mother respond to the child? Did she recognise the needs the child expressed and respond to them? Was she comfortable or uncomfortable on the ward? Was she co-operative; if not, is it possible to say why?

- *Helping the child and the parent*. It is important not to minimise the potential damage of separation from familiar surroundings, familiar care and familiar people around the child, particularly the main carer. Did Aaron have a favourite toy or comfort object? If the main carer is present, she should do the bulk of the caring for the child, maintaining his favoured routines. If as in this case, the main carer is also the alleged abuser, careful observation must occur to ensure that she does not harm the child further, and that the child *does* in fact prefer to be cared for by the parent, on the ward.

At this stage it is very important to remember that the bulk of children investigated for abuse *do* return home, even if a period of separation is required beforehand. This is why helping the child and helping the parent should if possible be undertaken together.

Parents involved in a child abuse investigation will usually feel threatened and often feel terrified (Cleaver and Freeman, 1995).

Ward staff can help parents continue to feel involved with and responsible for their child, so that if subsequent separation does occur, they can be encouraged to keep in contact with their child, which is an important factor in the child's eventual return home (Bullock *et al.*, 1993).

Aaron was discharged 24 hours after his admission to the care of his maternal grandmother, with both parents' agreement, prior to a child protection conference being called. His parents were in contact with Aaron, supervised by the grandmother.

At the child protection conference his name was placed on the child protection register in the category of physical injury. The medical reports and observations from ward staff had been particularly important in the discussions. The mother who attended the conference said ward staff had been very helpful and encouraging to her, and that she had felt very upset and anxious, but with their understanding had been able to look after Aaron on the ward.

The child protection core group was the social worker and the health visitor.

After three weeks Aaron was allowed home with his parents. Monitoring and assessment was carried out by social services. Both parents were very antagonistic to the social worker and reluctant to co-operate. The relationship with the health visitor, however, was excellent. She had worked with the family since Aaron's birth and knew the extended family who lived locally.

In her health surveillance role she was able to monitor Aaron's development, and gauge the likelihood of injury and harm. She was also able to support, encourage and provide advice to the parents, so that they were more prepared to take up services offered to them. She was also able to discuss the harm to Aaron from their warring lifestyle. The parents had thought that Aaron was much too young to be affected by their fighting.

Case 2

Jodie is ten, black British, and is the oldest of four children. She is a mature and some would say, prematurely competent young girl. Her mother is very loving towards all her children. She is a single parent who has mild learning disabilities and leans on Jodie for support. Jodie no longer has contact with her father. Every so often Jodie's mother feels she cannot cope and the children are looked after by friends or the local authority. The home is usually tidy and well organised, but there is a constant stream of friends and acquaintances passing through.

Jodie was sexually assaulted by a white man known to Jodie's mother who had offered to take her out. Jodie told her mother immediately after the assault and her mother contacted social services. There was insufficient evidence for this man to be prosecuted.

What losses is Jodie suffering? Before the assault she was already experiencing some loss of the normal expectation of a relatively carefree childhood. Her home life was not stable and she felt herself responsible for monitoring her mother's coping abilities, supporting not only her mother but her siblings too. She has also lost a stable father figure to relate to.

Since the assault, Jodie has lost more of her childhood, her sexual innocence. There is no physical damage, but she has experienced a severe dent in her emerging positive image of herself as a young black girl. She feels guilty and responsible, and unclean. She is also very frightened that the abuser might find her again.

At home her behaviour is difficult and defiant, her mother is finding it hard to cope with her, but feeling extreme guilt about what happened.

At school Jodie has lost her concentration and is disruptive in class. Jodie confided in a friend about the abuse and now she is teased and children are shouting out in the playground that she has AIDS.

Jodie's school has a link with a school nurse who is available one morning a week for parent or child consultations. The nurse was able to discuss what had developed into a fear of AIDS with Jodie and her mother together and to hear what Jodie and her mother had to say about additional bullying at school. The nurse became a confidante and support to both Jodie and her mother over the next two weeks and also:

- formed a bridge between Jodie's mother and the class teacher, with whom Jodie's mother felt ill at ease at this stage, because of her loss in confidence as a parent because of the assault. The bullying was addressed.
- with mother's consent informed the family health visitor about Jodie's mother's parenting struggles and a particular anxiety in relation to how she would cope when Jodie started to menstruate. The health visitor was then able to deal with this issue and provide a further support for the family.
- with mother's consent contacted Social Services to reinforce the urgency for therapeutic help for Jodie and her mother (they were already on a waiting list for help).

This brief intervention was helpful and supportive to Jodie and her mother and went some way to ameliorating and making sense of the problems at school brought on by the abuse. It also provided a non-stigmatising support figure for Jodie (and her mother) which could be useful in the future.

Although Jodie had, as far as is known, only suffered one assault, her trauma reaction was extreme. But because the problems were identified quickly, and her difficult behaviour understood, it was possible to provide help and encourage her mother to support Jodie, so important for her long-term recovery. The effects of her mother's inability to always provide care for her daughters was in many ways a more difficult problem for Jodie that would not be helped through brief intervention.

Points of Contact with Nursing Professionals

These are:

- identification of abuse or harm;
- referral;
- investigation;
- assessment;
- monitoring;
- family support.

The two detailed case studies have shown how health professionals can work from the point of investigation, to help the child and family, and gain a better understanding of the meaning of the abuse and harm to the child. Using the same attitudes and values this work can be done even earlier at the point of identifying abuse or harm and later through ongoing family support, leading to a greater sensitivity to the child's needs.

Practice Points to be Borne in Mind at All Stages of the Work

1. Making sense of the child's experience

- Understand the nature of the abuse, and the likely harm to the child resulting from this.
- Bear in mind all the different losses the child is suffering, not just the abuse.

- Understand the child in his or her particular context, e.g. the child's age and developmental stage, the birth family and other important people for the child, the child's race, culture and religion, any disability or particular health problems etc.

2. Skills and values

- Monitor the child's health, well being and development, or any injuries.
- Observe the child.
- Observe relationships.
- Listen to the child.
- Accept loss and ambivalence – one's own and the child's.
- Helping parents and carers helps children.

3. Working together

- Work together, but know and value your own professional role.
- Acknowledge the cumulative anxieties for professional workers as losses pile up.

References

American Psychiatric Association (1987) *Diagnostic and Statistical Manual of Mental Disorders*, 3rd edn (revised), DSM-111-R. Washington D.C.

Audit Commission (1994) *Seen But Not Heard*. London: HMSO.

Boat, B. (1994) Treatment of traumatised children. Paper to the international conference: Violence in the Family, Amsterdam, The Netherlands.

Bullock, R., Little, M. and Millham, S. (1993) *Going Home: The Return of Children Separated from their Families*. Dartmouth: Dartington Social Research Unit.

Cleaver, H. and Freeman, M. (1995) *Parental Perspectives in Cases of Suspected Child Abuse*. London: HMSO.

Department of Health (1991) *Working Together under the Children Act 1989: A guide to arrangements for inter-agency co-operation for the protection of children from abuse*. London: HMSO.

Draijer, N. (1994) Major developments in research in the long-term sequelae of child sexual abuse. Paper to the international conference: Violence in the Family, Amsterdam, The Netherlands.

Farmer, E. and Owen, M. (1995a) *Child Protection Practice: Private Risks and Public Remedies* London: HMSO.

Furniss, T. (1991) *The Multi Professional Handbook of Child Sexual Abuse*. London: Routledge.

Mrazek, D. and Mrazek, P. (1985) *Child Maltreatment* In: Rutter, M. and Hersov, L. (Eds), *Child and Adolescent Psychiatry*, 2nd edn. Oxford: Blackwell.

NCH Action for Children (1994) *The Hidden Victims: Children and Domestic Violence*.

Thoburn, J., Lewis, A. and Shemmings, D. (1995) *Paternalism or Partnership? Family Involvement in the Child Protection Process*. London: HMSO.

9
Protection and Loss: The Impact of Separation on the Abused and Neglected Child

Gillian Schofield

Children who come from families where they have experienced some form of abuse or neglect will have a wide and varied number of emotional and behavioural problems. These children may be separated from their family following child protection procedures and court decisions or because parents have reached the point where they do not feel they can cope with a child at home. Whatever the circumstances, at the point of separation the child will experience a profound sense of loss. Although it is to be hoped that the outcome in the long term will be positive for the child, we should never underestimate the range of losses which occur or the complexity of the impact on the child. When thinking about the implications for those professionals who work with children suffering the double trauma of abuse and separation, we need to look in some detail at the meaning to children of grief and loss in these circumstances.

Factors in the Experience of Separation

Loss of attachment figures

In order to understand separation in this as in other situations, it is important to understand the idea of attachment. The concept of attachment was developed largely in response to attempts to understand the impact of loss. As Bowlby has put it,

> Attachment theory is a way of conceptualising the propensity of human beings to make strong affectional bonds to particular others and of explaining the many forms of emotional distress and personality disturbance, including anxiety, anger, depression, and emotional detachment, to which unwilling separation and loss give rise (1979, p. 127).

A key element in attachment theory is the process by which young children build a relationship with an adult who can act as a secure base. It is this which enables a child to face new situations, build new relationships and cope with stress. When children experience stress, they turn to an attachment figure for help and comfort. This is part of normal development. When the cause of the stress is the loss of an attachment figure, the child may not know where to turn. It will be particularly hard for the child to make sense of what has happened. If a child is bereaved, there will be a period of working through strong emotions and coming to terms with the idea of death as well as separation. After divorce, the child will need help to understand the breakdown in the parents' relationship. For the child who comes into foster or residential care and loses an attachment figure following neglect or abuse and as a result of the decision of a court, it may be very hard to understand the reason for this separation.

Children, according to Fahlberg (1994), have different ways of understanding the loss. They may think that they have been *taken away* from their parents or kidnapped. This threatens their sense of confidence in their parents' power to protect them and makes children very anxious. Alternatively, they may fear that they have been *given away* by their parents, as if they are not good enough. This explanation is likely to make a child feel sad or depressed. They may believe that *they have brought about* the loss of the parent by something they have done. This would add to a child's feelings of responsibility for all subsequent events. All of these ways of trying to make sense of the situation can damage a child's self-esteem. These ideas may also cause the child great anxiety, but it is often the case that the child will not communicate these feelings directly to the new carers. As Fahlberg (1994) points out, children do not always share their anxieties or their magical thinking with adults. Children are far more likely to demonstrate behaviour difficulties which need care to understand.

Being separated from an attachment figure and placed in a strange foster home or children's home can make a child feel very much alone. We know that children whose relationship with parents has been difficult and stressful may have an insecure attachment and that paradoxically this can intensify the anxiety of the child (Ainsworth *et al.*, 1979). If a child has a secure attachment to a parent, then the child will have an internal model of a good parent which will encourage trust in a new carer, even though distressed. The child with an insecure attachment may be more inclined to cling desperately even to an abusive parent and will be less likely to accept the care of another adult. This factor is of course in addition to what is a natural feeling of loyalty, shared identity and belonging to the birth family and simply a wish that things will get better.

A more complex idea is that abused children may experience feelings towards their parents akin to those feelings experienced by people held as hostages towards their captors. When a child feels a sense of complete powerlessness in relation to an adult, there is a tendency to imbue the powerful adult with human qualities and values which make your own survival more likely. Thus the abused child may see the abusive adult or parent as having certain qualities and may find ways of explaining and excusing the parent's behaviour. The child's experience of separation from that adult will therefore be a very uneasy mix of relief and loss.

It may happen that a child is separated not only from adults who may represent a risk to the child but also from other people with whom there are significant relationships, such as siblings or grandparents. The importance of sibling relationships in particular is often overlooked. These relationships may not be particularly harmonious but they may have become an element of continuity and shared history which if the sibling group is separated in different foster homes or if one child is in care and the siblings are at home can leave the children feeling disorientated and distressed. As Dunn (1993) has described, siblings can also provide secure attachment figures, especially for young children. Friendships too can be very important for children in difficult family circumstances, and to lose these friendships when coming into foster care can also make children worried that their friends may think they have deserted them. What must be acknowledged is that these children will go through a grieving process which, as Aldgate has put it:

> may also include some or all of the following emotions: shock, alarm, denial and disbelief, yearning and pining, searching, anger or guilt, disorganisation, despair and, finally, reorganisation and integration (Aldgate and Simmonds 1988 p. 38).

Children will not be able to work through this process unless workers understand the complexity of this kind of loss. Being aware of the importance of siblings and friends, for example, can assist the worker in getting closer to the child and beginning to understand what that particular child's experience is.

The experience of abuse or neglect

Where children have experienced abuse or neglect, the nature of their experiences will affect their view of the separation. These examples illustrate how abusive experiences and patterns of relationships affect the nature of the loss.

> Sally, a 13-year-old black girl, had been physically and sexually abused over a number of years by her stepfather. She had been too frightened to tell anyone. Although she was greatly relieved to be safe in foster care she missed her younger half brother who was still at home and felt guilty about involving social workers in the family. She suffered anxiety about the welfare of her brother, who had also been physically abused.

> Patricia, a six-year-old with learning difficulties, had told teachers through her drawings and verbally about the fact that her father was sexually abusing her and that she wanted it to stop. When she was taken into care, she was completely unable to make the connection between what she had said and her removal from home. She settled without apparent protest in the foster home but seemed rather detached, not making relationships in the foster home.

> Donna, a nine-year-old girl, had been neglected because of her mother's serious alcohol problem. Donna had spent many brief spells in foster care when her mother couldn't care for her and she had witnessed violence. Finally she said that she wanted to stay with foster carers until her Mum stopped drinking. She felt very anxious about her mother and needed to see her regularly to check if she was alright.

Martin, a four-year-old boy, had been badly emotionally and physically neglected. His ability to express his feelings verbally was
very limited. In foster care, he continued to soil and smear faeces
as he had at home. He killed the foster family's hamster. He clung
to any adult he met, but was unable to form a secure attachment
with anyone.

What is clear from these examples, is that in different ways children
bring with them aspects of their past, whether it be disturbed
behaviour or feelings of anxiety and guilt. The reactions to the loss
must be seen in that context.

However, although there are links between reactions to loss and
reactions to abuse, it is very important for health and social work
professionals to distinguish between them. The child who has experienced physical abuse because of temporary severe stress in the
family, may also bring the loss of a good relationship. Sometimes
the powerful grief reactions to separation of a child in foster care,
are wrongly seen as evidence of abuse in the birth family. This is a
description given in an assessment report of the reactions of a
22-month-old boy in foster care as a result of bruises.

'Patrick's reactions in foster care showed signs that he had suffered
from emotional abuse. He didn't like his bottom being changed. He
soiled himself when the foster carer undressed him. He had difficulty sleeping and kept crying out in his sleep. He did not play
when the foster mother tipped out the toys and kept putting them
back in the box. He had a habit of hitting the side of his head over
and over again with such force that the foster mother had to
restrain him. After access he had a disturbed night. The foster
mother found him huddled in the corner of his cot.'

There could be a number of ways of understanding this behaviour.
He could indeed have been emotionally as well as physically
abused. However, two months prior to this, Patrick had been
developmentally checked by the general practitioner while with his
parents and was described as a happy, smiley child who was
developing normally. Other evidence confirmed that he was well
cared for. At the time he was physically abused by his stepfather,
his mother was in hospital having a second child and the family
were in poor accommodation waiting to be rehoused. His reactions
in the foster home were very similar to those shown in the Robertson films made in the 1940s on which Bowlby later built much of
his attachment theory (Bowlby, 1969). Patrick was overwhelmed
with anxiety and his behaviour regressed. He went through a phase
of despair. In time, Patrick accepted warmth from his foster carers.
Rather than seeing this as another phase in working through grief,
he was deemed to be responding to a relationship for the first time.

Although he did return home, his name was placed on the Child Protection Register under the category of emotional as well as physical abuse.

Loss of familiar surroundings

Children can find the change of environment very stressful. They are concerned that their old home has simply disappeared. As well as the sense of loss of the old there are difficulties in adjusting to the new and the unfamiliar. Young children who are just able to walk round the furniture at home become disorientated. Children who are just becoming more able to be independent by getting their own breakfast find themselves in a strange kitchen where nothing seems to be in the right place. Even teenagers find that it threatens their new found sense of identity to be away from the bedroom which has been carefully covered with the things which reflect that identity.

> Ian, aged two, was on the Child Protection Register under the category of neglect. He was placed in a foster home because his mother was due to give birth and needed the occasional break. The foster home was a long way from his own home and was a very different kind of house. He became very distressed and smeared faeces over his cot and on the walls. When he still failed to settle after several weekends, he was moved to a foster home on the estate next to where he lived. His mother pushed him to the foster home in the buggy rather than being driven by the social worker. The house was very similar to his own and the view from the living room window was almost identical. The sense of having been taken to a different world was much diminished and he showed none of his previous distress.

Race, culture and expectations

Children gain their confidence not just from attachment figures and familiar environments, but also from their culture. This may be as a result of belonging to a particular ethnic group. It may depend on commitment to a particular religion. The debate about the need for same race placements has highlighted this issue, but clearly whatever the long-term outcome, for the child placed in a family from a different ethnic or cultural background there are additional losses and greater challenges involved in coming to terms with separation from family and friends. This is so not only because of the loss of familiar culture and role models but also because ways of communicating feelings, including feelings of loss, may be different. Expressing feelings to a stranger may be seen as disloyal to one's family, making eye contact may be seen as disrespectful and so on. Thus the assessment of that child or young person's state of mind may be entirely wrong unless these factors can be taken into account. What we see as universal psychological processes may be experienced very differently and expressed very differently.

Family culture

In addition to broad cultural groups, each family has its own particular ways of doing things and its own values. Going to a new home can confuse the child as much with the different expectations as with the different environment. Eating a meal sat at a table may feel strange and formal. The sense of loss and unfamiliarity may make the child anxious about getting things wrong. 'Does this family get dressed before they have breakfast or afterwards?' 'Am I supposed to have a wash?' 'Can I get myself a drink?' Often in a panic about what to do, a child may take food secretly or hide dirty underwear behind the furniture. Getting these things wrong may risk the child feeling labelled as dirty or untidy. Such things are very stressful and compound the feelings of loss. However difficult the home environment may have been it probably still, from the child's point of view, had a predictability and was after all the only world the child knew.

Age and developmental stage

In thinking about any loss and separation for children, the age and developmental stage of the child will clearly be significant. For children looked after by the local authority, age and stage may be critical. As a child starts to form attachments during the first year of life, moves can be particularly problematic. If the move is from a poor relationship with a post-natally depressed mother into a secure relationship with a foster carer, the work towards returning the child to the mother needs to be planned to take both relationships into account. Bridging attachments will also be important if a child moves into an adoptive home.

For pre-school children beginning to gain a sense of autonomy and identity, the balance between age-appropriate dependency and independence will be disrupted as they cope with the stress of getting their dependency needs met by a strange adult.

School-age children are able to talk through some of their anxieties, but of course they are coping with the challenges outside the home. Grief and anxiety will take up energy so that school work and peer group relationships will suffer.

Teenagers – like pre-school children – are working on their identity and are separating out emotionally from parents, so for them to experience an abrupt separation in acrimonious circumstances leaves them struggling to make new relationships when developmentally they are thinking of asserting greater autonomy.

Issues for Professional Practice

As children go through the child protection system, they come across a wide range of professionals. Some will be closely involved with the child, such as key social workers and health visitors. Others may have regular contact without actually taking responsibility within the child protection system, such as teachers and school nurses. Others again may come across the child in the course of a busy working day, but are nevertheless significant in the child's life, such as the paediatrician during a ward round or the child care nurse during a hospital admission. For all these professionals certain important themes emerge from our analysis of these particular experiences of loss and grief.

Observing children

The subtleties involved in the child's behaviour when abuse and neglect are followed by separations mean that all professionals involved need to keep a very close eye on children so that they are not responding only to part of the picture. The need for careful observation of children may seem obvious but it is easier said than done. Whether there are serious injuries or concerns about emotional neglect, procedures for child protection tend to lead to a lot of rushing about as professional workers endeavour to investigate, assess, collect information, work appropriately with the parents and so on. Although social workers are likely to carry the main burden of responsibility for the investigation, nursing professionals are also likely to be involved and have an important contribution to make. The health visitor may no longer have the same involvement once a young child is in foster care even though their detailed previous knowledge may be vital if the child's behaviour in foster care and reaction to separation is to be understood. The nurse on the children's ward may have patients who are acutely ill, so that the neglected child who may have been admitted mainly for social reasons will not be a priority, even though the opportunity to follow through the child's eating patterns and response to stimulation and play may be central to an understanding of the child's needs.

Observation of behaviour needs to be able to incorporate a strong sense of the child's emotional responses as well as other indicators of development. The professional network can only too easily be making assessments based on partial information. This means that the help offered may prove ineffective.

Listening to children

Closely allied to the skill of observation, lies the skill of listening. Both require the practitioner to be receptive to the reality of the child's experience – both have active and passive elements. Children will not share their feelings unless the environment is right. This means that the worker has to make time for the child, create a sense of a private place and give the message that however feelings are expressed they will be listened to. Whether it is the need to confide anxieties about the abuse itself, or the need to talk about the happy memory of a father who may have abused the child, the culture must be one of acceptance. Complete confidentiality cannot be offered where children may be at risk, but developing trust is essential.

Communicating with children

These troubled children often have a sense that they have no control over their lives. For children to regain some trust in their environment, they need adults to give them as much information as they can reasonably understand. This may be about tests or procedures which they are undergoing (Wynne, 1992) or about ordinary details of the day's routine (Jewett, 1994). If adults can help children put even ordinary things into words and start to feel more in control then the process can start by which they begin to face more difficult feelings and put them into words.

Accepting loss and ambivalence – one's own and the child's

As Claudia Jewett says,

> Even in peripherally involved adults, a child's loss strikes a deep chord, triggering strong feelings left over from past losses, separations or rejections of their own (Jewett, 1984, p. 2).

In order to listen to children, awareness of one's own reactions to certain powerful emotions is very important. It is hard for professionals working with children coping with all sources of separation and loss to find the right words and to face their own memories. Professionals coming into contact with children about whom there have been child protection concerns have to deal with an extremely complex situation in which the child's feelings of grief and loss can easily be overlooked in the need to establish how best to protect the child. Where children have experienced certain kinds of abuse leading to separation, feelings run high, as these examples demonstrate.

> Peter, aged 18 months, was admitted to hospital with severe scalding to his feet and ankles from being lowered into a bath of very hot water. Mother and stepfather had been in the house at the time but neither was admitting responsibility or blaming the other. For the nursing staff, Peter's distress was hard to deal with. Being accustomed to working with sick children, they were accustomed to helping to alleviate pain, but the fact that the pain had been deliberately inflicted by a parent was an extra factor. It was hard to think that such things can happen when you work everyday with parents who are distraught at the pain their sick children experience. These feelings were then compounded by the fact that Peter's mother visited every day, and Peter was clearly very pleased to see her and cried when she left. Staff treated her with the respect and support they would offer any parent but the situation was a challenge to their professionalism. From Peter's point of view, he needed the nursing staff to keep the idea of his mother alive between visits as they would for other children, by talking about her, preparing him for each visit and helping him with his distress after visits.

> Sasha, aged 11 months, was brought to hospital suffering from failure to thrive and rickets. She was unable to hold up her head and was completely unresponsive to light or noise. She did not smile or communicate in any way. Nurses worked intensively with her and discovered that there was no physical cause for these developmental problems. It appeared that she had been left lying in her cot in a darkened room for long periods and had little experience of stimulation. Sasha's mother visited at intervals but Sasha failed to discriminate between her mother and other adults. The only sign of pleasure and recognition came when Sasha's older sister visited. Nursing staff were asked to give her appropriate

stimulation and she made good progress. They were also asked to encourage the mother to share the pleasure in Shasha's new abilities to smile and play because the plan was to attempt to return the child to her family.

When separated from family, children need practical help such as toys from home or photographs of parents in order to hang on to some sense of themselves. They also need sensitive adults to offer a relationship in which the child can feel safe to express feelings.

Where older children are concerned, they can express the ambivalence verbally. In a survey of young people's views of being in care, one young person said that she felt much safer in foster care and was well looked after but 'Nobody understands how much I miss my family, however bad living at home was' (Fletcher, 1993).

Working supportively with colleagues within nursing

When nursing professionals face these complex situations, they need to know that the stress and uncertainty can be contained in the staff group. Unlike other areas of nursing, medical expertise is rarely likely to resolve the problems facing the child. Even if there is a burn to be treated or a hungry child to be nourished, the family problems which brought the child into hospital or into foster care will continue. Peter and Sasha made good progress in hospital but their futures were still in the balance. The nurses on the ward faced the possibility that these vulnerable children might return home. The health visitor in the community may face the task of working with the parents during the reunification process. Where older children are concerned, the school nurse may find that the child who disclosed abuse is back at school and back at home.

Dealing with this very specialised area of work requires staff to feel that their concerns will be listened to by colleagues who understand their dilemmas so that they can continue to be sensitive to the fears and hopes of the children.

Working with colleagues in other professions

In order to offer appropriate help to children, communication between different disciplines is essential. This is such a common theme in child abuse inquiries, e.g. The Cleveland Report (Butler-Sloss, 1988) and Jasmine Beckford (Blom-Cooper, 1985), that we need to be clear about why it is so critical for these children. As Tattersall (1992) has pointed out, nursing professionals in particular can feel that their low status relative to paediatricians, for example, or their lack of knowledge of child protection relative to social workers, means that they are not as assertive as they need to be in contributing to the professional network. When the issue is around the child's ability to cope with abuse and separation, it may well be that nursing professionals have had more opportunity to get close to a child over time and they need to be assertive on behalf of the child.

As well as the issue of shared information, it is very likely that nursing professionals will feel some sense of responsibility for these children which is shared with other professionals. This responsibility for the child's sense of grief is very similar to that of a parent and invokes intense anxiety. As Woodhouse and Pengelly (1991) have demonstrated, the fear of being 'a bad parent' can affect individual practitioners but it also creates anxiety in multi-agency networks in child protection cases. The stress needs to be handled carefully so that the child is able to experience a sense of the professional network working together in their interest. Nothing is worse for the child's own anxiety level than to hear professionals criticising each other or to sense conflict and disagreements.

Conclusion

As Aldgate has suggested,

> intervention designed to effect mediation of the negative effects of separation and loss must be based on a fundamental belief that separation involves fear which needs to be mastered, and that loss involves grief which needs to be expressed (Aldgate and Simmonds, 1988, p. 44).

For children who experience violence, abuse or neglect, these feelings about separation take on a particularly complex form. It is necessary for all professionals who work with children who are separated from their families, in hospital or in substitute care, to acquire an understanding of these issues if they are to be able to apply their skills effectively to help children.

References

Ainsworth, M.D.S., Blehar, M.C., Waters, E. and Wall, S. (1979) *Patterns of Attachment: A Psychological Study of the Strange Situation*. Hillsdale, NJ: Erlbaum.

Aldgate, J. and Simmonds, J. (Eds) (1988) *Direct Work with Children*. London: BAAF.

Blom-Cooper, L. (1985) *A Child in Trust: Report on the Death of Jasmine Beckford*. London: HMSO.

Bowlby, J. (1969) *Attachment and Loss, Volume 1: Attachment*. London: Hogarth Press.

Bowlby, J. (1979) *The Making and Breaking of Affectional Bonds*. London: Tavistock.

Butler-Sloss, E. (1988) *The Report of the Inquiry into Child Abuse in Cleveland*. London: HMSO.

Dunn, J. (1993) *Young Children's Close Relationships: Beyond Attachment*. London: Sage.

Fahlberg, V. (1994) *A Child's Journey Through Placement*. London: BAAF.

Fletcher, B. (1993) *Not Just a Name*. National Consumer Council/Who Cares? Trust.

Jewett, C. (1984) *Helping Children Cope with Separation and Loss*. London: Batsford. (Revised 1994.)

Tattersall, P. (1992) Communicating assertively to protect children in nursing practice in C. Cloke, and J. Naish (Eds), *Key Issues in Child Protection for Health Visitors and Nurses*. Harlow: Longman.

Woodhouse, D. and Pengelly, P. (1991) *Anxiety and the Dynamics of Collaboration*. Aberdeen: Tavistock.

Wynne, J. (1992) The construction of child abuse in an accident and emergency department. In C. Cloke and J. Naish (Eds) *Key Issues in Child Protection For Health Visitors and Nurses*. Harlow: Longman.

10
Staff Care and Support

Elizabeth Capewell and Lilian Beattie

Children and their families dealing with loss and grief can find themselves being cared for by a wide range of professionals and carers, who themselves need to be supported. These include medical and health care professionals; educationalists – teachers, educational welfare officers, educational psychologists; social workers; staff in children's homes; volunteers from organisations such as CRUSE, Compassionate Friends, Samaritans; specialist support groups (for example CLIC – Cancer and Leukaemia in Childhood); foster parents; private counsellors and therapists. Attention must be drawn to the special tension that parents find themselves in. They are both carers and part of the wider supporting community which 'contains' the grieving child that is in need of care. Special strategies are needed by them in managing that tension and in dealing with helpers who find this dual role hard to handle. When children are dealing with loss and grief associated with divorce, the parents may also have the role as perpetrators of the distress as well as being carers and in need of care.

In this chapter, the needs of carers will be considered and suggestions offered for strategies that can be used to ensure that they can give the best possible support to children suffering from loss and grief. Formal and informal approaches to staff care within an organisation will be discussed along with self-help methods and specialist sources of support. This chapter should be read in conjunction with Chapter 5 which deals with organisational responses and suggests the context and culture in which staff care can flourish.

Aims and philosophy of staff care

The purpose of staff care is threefold: primarily to ensure that the children receive a good service and are protected from staff who are unfit emotionally, physically and professionally; secondly to ensure that the stress of the work does not have a detrimental effect on the health of staff; and thirdly to reduce costs to the organisation of litigation, high staff absenteeism and turnover, and low morale. If the staff do not feel cared for, they will be less able to provide good care for the children and families with whom they work. Essentially, staff care is about supporting and empowering carers to support and empower the child to deal and cope with his or her own distress – no one can or has the right to take anyone's experience from them by ignoring it or being over-protective. Like a Russian doll: each doll is held and supported at the base by the larger doll, but each doll has its own space and is a doll in its own right. Being a carer or the supporter of a carer does not give anyone the right to have power over another – all should be equal partners in the care of the child – including the child. Recognition that all children have different needs is paramount, especially if the child is regressing and expressing an inability to cope. Information needs to be based on the experience and situation of the child, and must be offered creatively and with sensitivity.

Why do carers need care and support?

Carers come into the helping professions with a whole range of motives, attitudes and ambitions. As the ideals and expectations of the early vocation to care become jaded by the pressure of the work, the issues of the organisation and other life stresses, more negative aspects come into play. They manifest in staff burn-out, cynicism, over-involvement, retreat into procedures and rules, low morale and poor health. Inevitably, poor performance results if staff members have no energy left to care for others or they do so in unhelpful ways.

The role of carer is a complex emotional interaction between people, especially where the power differences between carer and cared for are unacknowledged. Carers have to be helped to do this and reduce the differences, especially because they are working with children and with families in crisis. People in crisis may already feel they have lost control. They are vulnerable and emotionally exposed. Thus they are open to the more degenerate aspects of caring such as manipulation and control which would keep them in the role of victim. Kfir's (1989) definitions of elements found, to varying degrees, in all our characters are useful in understanding how the caring relationship can go awry. In an attempt to avoid rejection, insignificance, ridicule and stress, we develop attitudes and behaviour which can develop into any of four strategies. In a caring role these can be detected in:

Pleasing: self-sacrifice beyond the call of duty and the needs of the child; invasion of privacy; need for gratitude; inability to let go of the child. The child has to please the carer in order for the carer to survive.

Moral superiority: martyrdom; the need to know more; to be better and wiser so that the child's own wisdom and knowledge of themselves is denied.

Control: ensuring that everything is kept under a tight rein so that nothing can go wrong or upset the equilibrium. Thus there is no room for a child to expose chaotic thoughts, feelings and behaviour.

Avoidance: denying difficult situations and conflicts, such as the raw feelings of a child who is grieving or the reality of death. Some situations and children may actually be physically avoided altogether. Other strategies include telling the child they are being brave when they need not to be or by finding the silver lining in their cloud before the darkness of their cloud has been recognised.

Many carers also get caught in the trap of being so concerned with how they will appear to the child, whether they will be good enough, or what they can get from the situation, that they are not really present for them at all. A less stressful and, for the child, a more effective stance is to enter the relationship saying: What can I contribute to this person in this situation?

Carers often find that they will begin to feel and behave in a way that mirrors the issues facing those being cared for. Feelings, positive and negative, are contagious and may trigger reactions in the carer. Because these reactions may be more relevant to a past situation, carers need to be aware of this process. Otherwise the care becomes inappropriate for the current situation.

Carers of children are more open to having their own existential fears triggered for all the reasons described in Chapter 5 relating to the myths and taboos surrounding children in distress. If the carers are not helped to be aware of these fears and other neurotic traits then they will not be able to offer what the children really need and they certainly will not be able to help them through their loss. If, for example, a carer fears death, then they will fear talking to children openly about death and will not be able to support them through a loss experience.

Such traps are common for all carers, but for those who care for children they are potentially more dangerous. They are having to care for someone who is dependent on others, their parents, who have rights over the child and are probably feeling keenly that they have lost control over what is happening to their child. All adults involved are trying to interpret what the child wants and needs and what is in his or her best interests. With older children and especially adolescents, the problems increase. They have minds of their own but decision making may be impaired by the loss, medication, insufficient information, lack of experience, and whatever independence/dependence games are being played out.

It must also be remembered that it is only recently that the real experience of children who are grieving has been understood and strategies for supporting them developed. Carers of children are often marginalised, under-resourced and disbelieved, mirroring attitudes in society towards children. Their work is therefore difficult in its content and context, and personal and professional aspects of the carer are challenged unremittingly.

For all these reasons all carers and especially carers of children must be cared for and supported to keep up their ability to care. There needs to be a base level of everyday care and this needs to be supplemented at times of unusual distress, such as major disaster or where the organisation or carer is undergoing change and stress.

Signs of carer stress

The normal reactions that carers may experience as a result of stressful incidents in their work are:

- fear over professional competence, responsibilities and legal liabilities;
- guilt over perceived 'inadequacies';
- feelings of helplessness;
- anger at the situation;
- urge to rescue;
- distrust of the department or system;

- reminders of personal issues;
- doubt, confusion and neediness.

Entering into a relationship with grief-stricken, depressed or traumatised children and their families carries risks. The reactions may not be dramatic enough to warrant medical attention, but they are enough to make life miserable for the carer and people close to them. Carers can end up becoming:

burnt out	irritable
depressed	alienated
suspicious	cynical
cold/unfeeling	suicidal
difficult to live and work with	pessimistic
anxious	despairing
distrustful	

Often it is family, friends and colleagues who notice the changes and will be snapped at irritably if they mention them to the carer! Where the incident is particularly difficult, the carer may mirror the acute and delayed reactions of those he or she is caring for such as poor concentration, nightmares, depression and psychosomatic aches and pains. Dealing with very distressed children can be frightening. It takes a special energy, and raises feelings and unfinished personal business that other caring situations do not.

No one doing this work can remain unmoved by it. Where carers are constantly experiencing exceptionally stressful work, especially if they feel unvalued by the organisation, symptoms of cumulative stress may develop, characterised by more subtle symptoms such as:

- loss of hope;
- loss of purpose;
- loss of feeling in control;
- loss of connection;
- loss of integrity.

These all contribute to a feeling of apathy and loss of energy which could be described as a 'depletion of the spirit' (Johnson, 1993). These reactions are difficult enough in themselves without support but they may be made worse by the carers themselves if they choose to counter them with maladaptive measures such as over-use of drink and drugs, bingeing/starving and other addictive/compulsive behaviours; withdrawal; and impulsive life-style changes. These can lead to a downward spiral causing relationship problems and difficulties at work.

The equation:

[Chronic stress + Traumatic stress + Maladaptive measures =
Cumulative stress]

is a very dangerous situation for carers and it is this that support
for carers aims to prevent.

What is 'being cared for'?

In caring for carers, what interventions are available? Caring isn't
simply being nice to someone or giving reassurance that all will be
well. Though listening and reassurance may be all that is needed in
some cases, it can be very frustrating telling your story over and
over again without being facilitated to move on if that is what is
needed. Caring may need to include some more rigorous interventions which enable clarification of boundaries, abreaction of emotions, challenging examination of motives, empowerment, and the
development of skills.

The following case histories illustrate some of the needs of carers
and the range of interventions which can be used.

1. A head teacher of a junior school had to deal with the impact
of a house fire which killed two of his pupils and their mother.
Many other pupils and their parents had been involved in the
rescue attempts, had heard the screams or had seen the recovery
of the bodies. Many parents and the dead children's father sought
help from the school and the Head in particular.

What support and care did the Head need?

His needs were to:

*   function in his normal role as Head;
*   function in the extra role as supporter of parents, staff and
    children;
*   facilitate the mourning process and rituals in the school.

To fulfil all these exhausting roles he needed to:

*   deal with his own feelings and reactions about the deaths and
    his responsibilities;
*   deal with the reactions of staff and mobilise their support;
*   have skills and information to deal with the reactions of pupils
    and parents;
*   have skills and clarity to mobilise support from external agen-
    cies;
*   be informed about personal, group and community reactions
    to critical incidents in general and in relation to this event.

Support had to be personal, managerial, organisational, psychological and practical. All school staff needed stress debriefing and information before they could be effective with the children. The range of interventions open to the Head and staff could therefore be:

- personal stress debriefing and consultancy from managers and a specialist consultant to deal with personal issues and professional responses;
- staff group debriefing or meeting to share reactions, be given common facts of what happened and what will be done, and mobilise support;
- information on trauma, bereavement and grief;
- individual or group supervision to develop skills and monitor the responses to children and parents;
- on-going support for the Head and key staff while dealing with the long-term impact;
- organisational support prior to the incident in the form of training and preparation for managing crises and dealing with loss and grief would reduce the stress of uncertainty about how to respond.

2. A 9 year old boy had been moved from one primary school to another because of his behaviour. At first he settled into the new school without problems but within weeks his work and behaviour deteriorated. The staff thought he was just being naughty but the Head began to suspect that there was more to it than that and so sent him to see the school doctor for further tests. The boy was found to be suffering from a degenerative illness and he was expected to die within two years. (Three years later he is still alive and in need of 24-hour-a-day care.) The school doctor explained to the boy simply that something was happening inside him that was making him behave differently. His mother was also given a session of explanation and support by the doctor. The staff had to come to terms not only with the horror of the diagnosis and prognosis but also with their irritation at the boy and their incorrect assessment of the cause of his behaviour. They also had to deal with their feelings about the boy's mother, a single parent, and how she would pamper her youngest son.

What care did all these carers need?

Their needs were:

- initially someone who could discern that the real issue for them was that their opinions and judgements about the boy had been based on the assumption that he was physically normal;
- help in dealing with their reactions – especially feelings of guilt;
- practical help from other agencies.

The care arranged for them came mainly from the school doctor while the family were supported by health and social services. It took the form of:

- information about the boy's illness and prognosis;
- training and/or supervision to help them tell the other children about the boy and his illness;
- a group session for staff to help them understand the real issues affecting them – before they dealt with the boy, his mother and the other pupils.

The school doctor who had undertaken most of the care for the carers also talked through her feelings with her supervisor about the heartbreaking condition of the boy and the difficult job of telling him about his illness.

3. Children's Homes have to deal with some of the most intractable problems in difficult circumstances, often with the poorest resources and the least trained staff. This case history highlights the needs created by two different children in their care. Both children desperately wished to be reunited with their birth families and would not accept anything from the Home – the last place they wanted to be. They were extremely hostile and angry, though this was expressed in very different ways.

Child A, a boy aged 12, kept interrupting a meeting of professionals. He managed to take each one out of the meeting in turn and threw hostile, caustic remarks at them. To one he snarled, 'So you're the fat bitch who writes reports and gets kids taken away from their families.' At other times he stayed out all night, knocked down doors and attacked staff. When he got what he wanted he was perfectly charming. This boy had no feeling of belonging anywhere. The staff found him very difficult to manage and his behaviour was felt to be the cause of much of their stress and resulting absenteeism.

Child B, a girl, had been rejected by her mother and step-father. The girl's own father left when she was six. Her mother remarried and had two more children. The girl was seen to be disrupting the 'new' family and she was put into temporary care. They did not want her back. The girl was dealing with her anger by being compliant – a real little 'goody two shoes'. She desperately wanted to go home and could not understand why her family did not want her back. Others could not understand either why they did not want such a good girl back. Goodness was a mask to her hostility. Fostering was unlikely to have worked as she had built up such an idealised view of what a foster family would be like that it would never be good enough.

The problem for staff here was that they were dealing constantly with seemingly intractable problems and with children who not only may not have wanted their help but who also went out of their way to destroy the fabric and morale of the Home and the system of care. Thus the children themselves were destroying the support of an ordered working environment that others in stressful work can depend on. Many of the children for whom these staff are trying to care have no true sense of belonging and cannot make co-operative relationships, or can only do so in a limited way.

They are constantly negatively impinging on a system of order and any sense of social order. They are so hurt and humiliated by repeated rejection that they cannot allow anyone to take them in so they set themselves up to be rejected. Their belief that there is no place for them anywhere is reinforced.

What care did the staff in this Home need?

Their needs were:

- to deal with their own reactions to constant challenging behaviour and personal physical and verbal attacks;

- to deal with the mirroring effect – like the children they too may feel isolated, rejected, and marginalised, especially as they often have low status and pay in their profession and organisation;

- top quality information and skills to develop competence and confidence in handling difficult situations;

- systems which do their utmost to provide physical safety;

- regular encouragement, reassurance and recognition for the difficult role they have – especially from managers.

The type of care needed for these carers must be of the best quality and should include:

- opportunities for personal development to allow carers to strengthen their sense of self and deal with personal issues;

- regular group and individual supervision;

- excellent systems support especially in communications about the children, their backgrounds, needs and development;

- consultancy on the children and the purpose of their behaviour and opportunities to depersonalise what is happening to them and the children;

- help in creating intervention strategies that cut through the child's hostility and create a dynamic which demands co-operative behaviour from the child;

- joint supervision for all the key workers who have an involvement with each child to talk through concerns together, otherwise the child may play one worker off against another and exploit weaknesses in working relationships.

A few fortunate people have felt so supported and cared for from childhood that they have built this into their own internal world which ensures they receive all the care they need when they need it. At the other extreme, some staff are so needy that they will have unrealistic expectations of care from the organisation, colleagues and indirectly from the people they are caring for as well. Somewhere in the middle lies the majority with an adequate level of personal support and a varying degree of organisational support. Much of the time they may not notice what they have, how they get it, or how they give it.

People's need for caring, and their concept of being cared for, varies greatly from person to person. The quantity and type of care required are functions of past personal history, especially of being supported and cared for; other present life needs; the efficiency and appropriateness of current support systems; their expectations of care from family, friends, society and/or their organisation; the range of coping styles available to them; their personality type; the nature of the loss and grief they are dealing with. Care for the carer therefore needs to be carefully matched to the person and the situation. The wrong care at the wrong time by the wrong person can be worse than no care at all. Needs and expectations in any individual can vary at different times and in different situations. Carers who have coped for years may suddenly flounder if their job is threatened or a close friend dies and their own needs for care are not being met.

Support is not just about nodding heads and kind voices – it can be practical, physical, spiritual, emotional, and social. It can be given verbally or non-verbally, by an organisation, society, group, family, another individual, or to oneself. Offering one's experience, knowledge and insights to discern the needs, rather than the wants, of the carer is the best support that can be given. If it can also be given with wisdom and unconditional love, the carer will be able to survive anything that the work throws at him or her.

Legitimising staff care

A myth, common amongst those in the helping professions, is that to be in need of care oneself means that you should not be in the job. It prevailed amongst carers even in the period of incredible stress for staff after the Hillsborough disaster (Harper, 1993). This myth prevented many staff from asking for help. Only after a pro-active outreach strategy by the Staff Care Co-ordinator did people seek assistance formally, while others did so more indirectly. The training day she organised became an opportunity for mass sharing, debriefing and support which demonstrated just how great the needs were. The myth was held even more strongly by staff who were not in the front-line of care, such as managers and administrators, to the detriment of themselves and their staff.

Such a myth becomes fixed in an organisation by the policies and statements made about staff care. A cognitive shift needs to be made from regarding the need for care as a sign of weakness to recognising this as a sign of good management of one's reactions to the work. From our earliest experience we learn that giving and receiving are not always 'emotionally clean' gestures. They often come with many strings attached and we learn to distrust the exchange. Carers are often poor receivers of help, finding it preferable to be the givers. This can be very uncomfortable for the receivers of their care. The experience for carers of receiving care is therefore a valuable one, though they may need training in how to become good receivers.

Staff care: rights and responsibilities

No organisation can be held responsible for meeting all the needs of the staff, although Health and Safety requirements expect that staff will not be damaged by the working environment which increasingly includes stress. However, caring organisations will ensure good practice in appropriate selection procedures, induction, training and job descriptions to reduce uncertainty and stress. Many will also give staff access to occupational health professionals and counsellors. Their responsibilities will be limited to needs arising from the work itself, although some go further and offer help for personal issues which may affect performance. There is a point though where staff must also take responsibility for their own care, especially for personal issues from the past which continue to affect their reactions in the present. However, the organisation can still do a lot to encourage and support this. A person working excessive hours will not have the time or energy for caring for themselves.

Staff involved in unusually distressing work such as that created by major disasters have particular needs which may have to be enshrined as rights in order for their care to be organised and resourced. Staff involved in disaster work often have such a strong need for the organisation to acknowledge the intensity of the work that no amount of personal care will be sufficient until this is given. After major or other unusual events staff need, and have the moral right, to receive the following:

- acknowledgement that they are involved in highly stressful situations as part of their normal work role;
- that as a legitimate part of work they will be given help to deal with the stress that results;

- where the stress is significantly more than would normally be expected in their job that they will be given extra help as needed, including group stress debriefing if appropriate;
- that reparation or compensation will be given to help with any financial costs incurred by the impact of being involved;
- that the organisation will learn from their experience and build the learning into future policies and make it available for the good of others;
- that the organisation will support opportunities for the individual to pass on their learning to others thus demonstrating that their experience has been valued. (Capewell, 1992).

Staff care strategies

Employer led strategies: for individuals

Chapter 5 sets out the framework and environment required for good care of staff. In it the importance of supportive management policies and styles, staff induction, training and development to ensure up-dated competence in skills, information and attitudes was stressed. If these are not adequate for a basic job to be accomplished then it does not matter how much care is supplied in other ways, staff will always carry the feeling of being unsupported. This is most likely to happen in organisations where it is perceived that money is available for such things but where spending on staff care is not seen as a priority by managers, or where market forces or management styles are seen to be operating at the expense of concern for staff. A variety of specific care strategies are available.

Non-managerial supervision

Supervision helps carers to remember that 'good enough' work is as much in the being as the doing; as much in the attitude as the knowledge – and that they are themselves only humans doing extremely difficult work. In this case, the supervisor has no managerial responsibility for the carer so concerns and worries may be revealed without fear of being judged as incompetent. Supervision is mainly educative and supportive but even though it is non-managerial, supervisors still have responsibility for ensuring that carers are in a fit state to do their job without harming the children they are supporting. This system offers carers an opportunity to deal with all their uncertainties and the emotions triggered by their work or which interfere with their work. It also helps carers to be aware of the belief systems they have about themselves, the world around them and their place in it. Carers need to be secure in their sense of belonging where they are working with children who are vulnerable, depressed or abreacting, sometimes in extreme and unexpected ways. Supervisors of these carers need to encourage them to believe that they are doing their job and are sound people even if they feel terrible, make mistakes or if children do not respond in the way they feel they should. Supervision can be obtained in several ways:

Individual supervision. Supervision is given in a one to one setting by a supervisor from outside the organisation or from a different part of the same organisation.

Group supervision. Supervision is given by one supervisor to a small group of carers with similar or complementary roles. The group may be from the same organisation or chosen by the supervisees themselves. This form of supervision is also useful where several carers are looking after the same child, a joint approach helps to avoid one carer being played off against another.

Peer supervision/Co-supervision. In the previous types of supervision, the supervisor is given the power to take responsibility for conducting the supervision. Usually the supervisor has had special training in supervision skills and/or has greater knowledge or experience than the carer being supervised. With peer supervision all the supervisees have equal status and there is no one person who acts as supervisor. It may be conducted as a pair (co-supervision) or as a group. It is usually most successful where the peers are very experienced in reviewing their work and where they have equal confidence in supervising each other. Even so, training in peer supervision skills is advisable and some facilitation is helpful in setting up and reviewing the groups. The principles and practice along with the advantages and disadvantages of each type of supervision are clearly described in Hawkins and Shohet, (1989).

Internal confidential staff care

This involves using counsellors who are set apart from other departments in the organisation. These counsellors are usually managed by Staff Welfare or Occupational Health departments. Their success depends on the trust placed in them by staff and the way in which the service is made known to staff.

Cross agency specialist teams

As a response to staff needs following major or very traumatic incidents cross agency teams have been set up. In Lincolnshire for example, a team able to conduct Critical Incident Stress Debriefings has been drawn from each of the emergency services, health services and social services. No one ever debriefs anyone from his or her own service.

External systems such as Employee Assistance Programmes

Some organisations have contracted out their staff counselling to commercial organisations operating either a counselling service or a full Employee Assistance Programme. Any member of staff is able to contact a 24-hour help-line for telephone counselling or referral to a counsellor in complete confidence. Preventive education programmes add to the effectiveness of the service.

Employee led strategies

While employers should take their responsibilities for the care of their staff seriously, carers should also take their share of responsibility for their own care. They should ensure they are physically, emotionally and professionally fit for the post they are contracted to undertake. Some carers prefer to make their own arrangements for their support and care to supplement or replace what is provided at work. If costs are involved they will bear them personally and it will be done out of work time. Some prefer to pay for the benefits of having complete freedom from the organisation, especially where they mistrust confidentiality. Unfortunately, some carers find they are labelled as weak and incompetent if they seek particular kinds of support at work. The other advantage of private arrangements is that help can be sought in a more holistic way and need not be confined to the needs of work. There is also more freedom to seek help in more creative ways than may be available or possible in an organisation.

Personal supervision, consultancy, mentoring

It is still quite difficult to find good quality professionals to provide these forms of support at affordable prices but the search can be well worth the effort. It is best to ask for personal recommendations and to shop around. The person chosen does not have to be from the same profession or agency but he or she does need to have the correct skills, understand the organisational context of the work and be clear about boundaries and context. A successful relationship can provide a valuable mechanism for self and professional development since all the session is geared to the carer's needs and can help the carer adapt theoretical learning to the needs of his or her particular job.

Personal therapy / counselling

The same difficulties apply here to finding the right counsellor or therapist but the search itself can be a valuable learning opportunity. Some bodies such as the British Association of Counsellors have directories of their accredited counsellors and non-accredited counsellors who abide by their code of practice. For some specific problems such as phobias or depression it is worth checking with a GP to see what is available through the National Health Service. Some voluntary agencies operate a charging system related to means. The disadvantage of charitable and free services is that the carer does not have a choice about who he or she sees and this can be important in such a personal encounter. When choosing a counsellor or therapist it is worth bearing in mind that the type of counselling or therapy practised is often less important than the personal attributes, integrity and skills of the person practising it. How this person was trained and how he or she is currently supervised is important. The type of records that will be kept and who has access to these should be clarified. If the person chosen does not seem right, the carer should not be afraid to end the contract, remembering that most people can go through periods of anger or discomfort with their counsellor or therapist.

Self-supervision

The basis of all personal and professional development is the level of awareness of oneself and one's practice. Part of the aim of all other forms of support is to enhance this ability for self-supervision. The question that people working in all caring professions face is: Am I fit to do this work professionally, cognitively, emotionally, physically, behaviourally and spiritually? Work with children in loss and grief particularly challenges all these aspects of any professional. Preparation is the best defence against burn-out. Self-supervision needs discipline and commitment. It needs to be practised regularly but it does not need to take much time. Recording observations about incidents which have been particularly successful are as important as concentrating on those felt to be difficult or a failure. This can be facilitated through structured reflection using a recognised model such as that proposed by Gibbs (1988) or a series of questions devised by oneself and which focus thoughts on the time before, during and after the event. These questions might include: What was actually happening? Who was around? What were they saying and doing? What was I doing and saying? What was I thinking? What else was going on for me, at home and work, at the time? What words would describe how I was feeling? What was going on in my body (stiffness, aches etc.)? What interventions did I use? What else could I have done? What would I choose to do in future similar situations? Keeping a journal or recording events and feelings through drawing are other useful forms of self-supervision. The aim of all the methods is to sharpen one's powers of observation and to be clear about the facts. Strong emotions often cause people to distort what was really happening and thus their feelings and judgements about their performance also become distorted.

Self-development

Those who are most secure in their life and work are usually those who take full responsibility for themselves. They clearly know their rights and what they can expect from an organisation and also know they have the final responsibility for what they do and where they work. These are the people who have balanced lives and work to live rather than live only through their work. Though they are not immune from stress, they are likely to cope with it better, seeing difficulties as much a part of life as the good times. Self-development involves creating opportunities for different experiences, exploring different aspects of oneself, taking opportunities for training and professional development and seeking these out rather than waiting for them to happen. Those in very stressful roles may find it beneficial to prepare themselves for a complete change of career or a break in order to renew themselves. Even if a radical change is not possible, a change of location or role may also help. In any case each day should have some opportunity for contrast and recharging of the batteries, even if it is only a relaxing bath.

Networking

This is often an important mechanism of self-development. Networks vary in their formality – some are very structured with formal membership requirements, others are just left to happen when the need arises. They can be defined as groups of people with some common interest or aim who are accessible to each other for mutual support and development or exchange of ideas, skills and information. They often fulfil a social as well as professional function and can be conducted by phone, written word, computer, e-mail or in person. The growth of networking makes discrimination essential, especially for those who use them to fulfil needs for contact – if too many networks are joined, so much energy is used in networking there is none left for the job.

Legal support

This is increasingly important as society becomes more interested in litigation. Joining a Union or professional organisation is important for many reasons but is especially supportive when conflicts arise with an employer or client.

Conclusion

It is important to remember when creating self-care and support, that enough to function effectively is all that is needed. Care and support is not needed for its own sake. Most of the time most people cope, though they may need to be reminded of that fact. Carers need to be aware of what they really need, not what they think they ought to do. The most important strategy is to be aware of vulnerabilities and triggers to distress and to know who to call and say 'Help!'.

Team led methods (instigated either by employers or team members)

Any situation can be both a source of care and support or a source of stress. Nowhere is this more true than with teams. Where a team is compatible and pulling in the same direction it can provide a strong cradle of support which acts as a buffer to the most distressing work or the most stressful organisation. Where this is not the case, it can be as stressful as living in a dysfunctional family pulling down the morale of its members and adding to the stresses of the job.

Well-functioning and supportive teams will clearly know their purpose both as a team and as individuals in the team. Boundaries between roles and other teams will be clear and there will be mechanisms for resolving conflicts in an adult manner. Lines of authority will also be clear as will lines of communication which will be two-way. Team development and review will be valued and practised regularly. Where energy does not have to be wasted in petty squabbles, attention seeking and power games, there will be enough energy for team members to give genuine care and support to each other. Time and energy will also be available for all the important informal things which make team members feel valued and supported, such as when new members arrive and old ones depart or when there are events to be celebrated or recognised in the life of the team. Social events will happen spontaneously because they are wanted and not as a ploy to get people together. More formal team methods which care for carers include the following:

Joint team training. However beware of offering training days as a 'treat', a day out, or a reward – if the team needs a rest, give them a rest. It is not fair to the trainer either if the motives for the day are confused.

Reviews and defusing. These focus on the emotional impact of the work and take place at the end of a shift, session, week or term. Teachers, increasingly dealing consciously and sub-consciously with the emotions of large numbers of children daily, could particularly benefit from this kind of defusing.

Critical Incident Stress Debriefing. This is a planned and structured process, with built-in ground-rules to ensure safety. It should be reserved for teams or groups after the most distressing incidents. It should be given as part of a longer programme of crisis planning and education and should always be followed up by a team session and monitoring of individual needs and referral where necessary. The need for a stress debriefing and the composition of the group should be assessed by someone trained in this work and undertaken by trained debriefers. It is particularly devised for people with a common experience of the trauma and who are suffering normal stress reactions. Other interventions are available for severely distressed team members. The aims of a debriefing are:

- to provide a common factual understanding of what happened in the event and the subsequent response;
- to provide a safe structure in which emotional reactions can be identified and briefly expressed;
- to inform and educate about common reactions, self-help

techniques, how to avoid secondary trauma and when and where to seek further help.

This type of debriefing is not a therapy group or counselling session, nor is it an operational debriefing.

Caring for yourself: self-help techniques

There are many popular self-help books available so this section will give just a small selection of techniques. They will be placed in a framework of coping styles based on the work of Dr Mooli Lahad (1993) from the Community Stress Prevention Centre in northern Israel. His ideas have grown out of many years experience of working with teachers, health and social service professionals caring for children under chronic and acute stress and trauma.

Developing your range of coping styles: the BASIC-Ph model

The basic premise of this model is that people have the potential to communicate with the outside world by receiving, processing and reacting to information through six basic channels. Though we all have access to all these channels, we usually have our own coping profile in which two or three channels are dominant. The aim is to promote coping by making use of our most dominant channels, especially in times of crisis, but also to expand our range of coping skills by developing access to less used channels. In extreme stress our usual ways of coping may break down and we have to try new methods. As well as strengthening the carer's coping strategies, BASIC-Ph also helps the carer understand the functioning of the child and family and him or herself, and is an important starting point for future development. The model integrates the six most dominant psychological modalities, derived from the major schools of psychology. The six channels will be described and an example of a self-help technique using that channel will be given. It should be remembered of course that some techniques, notably the creative arts, cut across several channels – it depends on the purpose for which you are using it. Remember too that any method can be used creatively or negatively, for example activity can help a person regain their health and sense of control, but it can also be an avoidance for the distress of a situation. It is all a matter of degree and balance.

These belong to the spiritual dimension and are related to the personal system of values, religious beliefs, cultural values and customs. Because beliefs are closely bound to the meaning and purpose we give to life, death and suffering, they are easily challenged by loss and grief, especially where children are involved, and need to be reviewed and strengthened if we are to cope well.

A self-help technique using the beliefs channel: metaphoric rituals. An important expression of belief systems are the rituals and ceremonies designed to prevent denial, regulate mourning, celebrate what has been lost and allow the transition to a new order. One of the problems of being a carer is that you experience many losses yet are detached from them. It is not always possible or appropriate to be a part of the mourning rituals of the family and losses not involving death have no rituals at all. A useful self-help technique is therefore the skill of creating metaphoric rituals which reflect the pattern of traditional separation ceremonies and use symbolic objects to connect what or who is lost with what or who continues. A letter may be written to release feelings or deal with unfinished business and be shredded or burnt or buried with the symbolic object with as much ceremony as possible. Some kind of actual or symbolic memorial can be created to complete the ritual. This could be the placing of flowers in a vase, the planting of a tree or the drawing of a memorial. Other 'Belief' techniques include prayer, lighting a candle, regular meditation, and engaging on a quest for meaning.

Affect (Emotions)

It is surprising how many carers regard the expression of emotions as a reason for apology rather than a means of coping. Carers whose subconscious motive for caring is to control are also likely to deny their own emotions so that they are the 'strong' ones while the child and his or her family are the vulnerable, emotional ones in need of care. The expression of emotions is cathartic and helps to reduce stress. The appropriate sharing of emotions with the child and family also opens up communications between the carer and cared for, equalising the relationship and adding a human dimension to the encounter. It is vital that carers also deal with left-over, unexpressed emotions from their own past otherwise these may be inappropriately expressed in current situations. The 'clean as you go' motto for McDonald's staff is as appropriate for carers as it is for fast food outlet employees. The technique described below enables carers to check out which emotions are associated with the present and which are the left-overs from the past.

A self-help technique using the affect channel: 'feeling, felt, thought'. This technique is based on the thinking of David Bohm (1992) where thought is seen to be actively participating in forming perceptions, meaning and actions, and is about tracking the origins of emotions. It helps a carer to be more aware of the source of emotions so that these can be expressed in the correct context and connections can start to be made between past and present. The technique is also supportive, in that the carer is less likely to react inappropriately to a situation or decide on incorrect interventions, thus making matters worse for children and their families. It enables the carer to start thinking instead of reacting. Whenever you are feeling unusually distressed about a situation or you hear your words coming out with too great a force, stop and scan. Ask yourself: When was the last time I felt like this? Look at what was happening and look for any similarities with the current situation. Then ask: When was the first time I felt like this? The answer to this question is most often found in childhood. The unconscious memory is being reminded of this event by similarities in the present situation. By going back to childhood we are learning about attitudes to ourselves and the world which helped form our developing belief systems. The beliefs of childhood, if not re-examined and redefined from an adult view, are carried with us into adulthood. They condition our responses and motivate our behaviour. If a situation as a child made us feel powerless then the similar situation as adults may trigger the same sense of powerlessness and so disable us.

> A carer found she was becoming extremely agitated and angry about a particular child protection case. Her job was to be a listener to the child but she wanted strong action to be taken by statutory agencies to protect the child from her step-father. She was not in a position to take direct action about the situation and the agencies involved were doing what was needed. Through this scanning technique she discovered that the present situation took her back to a time when, as a child, she was distressed. Her distress was recognised but no one did anything about it. This fed into her belief system, which carried into adulthood, that when any child is distressed, someone should always take action. This reaction was both causing her stress and preventing her from doing the job that she was actually meant to be doing – that is listening to the child.

A wide range of techniques for expressing emotions are available, from throwing clay and banging cushions to the whole range of expressive arts and drama.

Social

Understanding about this channel draws principally from Alfred Adler's Individual Psychology, identifying social inclination and interaction as basic motives for psychological survival, and Erikson's 'stages of development' theories. Love, support and help from the family is fundamental to our personal growth. Belonging to other social groups and having a role to play can help people through times of crisis. Carers do however need to be clear about the strengths and weaknesses of their support systems as these can also be the source of stress. In some types of crisis new social systems, such as common concern support groups, may have to be discovered or created. Support systems have to be maintained, strengthened and reviewed if they are to work well for the carer. Lines of communication need to be kept open so that help can be asked for when needed and refused when not. The following exercise shows how this can be done.

A self-help technique using the social channel: mapping your own support. On a large sheet of paper, draw yourself in the middle. Next write or draw all the people who form your social support system, locating them on the paper according to how close or distant they feel to you. You can then make your map as graphic as you like by drawing different kinds of lines and symbols to show how strong the links and lines of communication are. You can also show where the barriers and blocks are, where the rocky ground and marshes lie. It is also useful to indicate the kind of support that each person can give. Those who give good support in 'normal' times may be useless in a major crisis or over certain issues. Such a map can remind you of what you really have available, which support is redundant, which needs strengthening and where the gaps need filling. In times of distress it is easy to feel isolated and that there is no help available. Your map will show you at a glance where it can be found.

Imagination

This channel can take us out of ourselves, providing a break from our distress and the means to escape from the limits of our standard thinking into creative thought. It allows a dialogue between all aspects of ourselves and allows space for our intuition. The dominance of imagination in our inner world was prominent in the Analytical Psychology of Carl Jung. He emphasised the relevance of symbols and archetypal images found in ancient mythology, legends, dreams and creative artwork and these are all important in the techniques which use this channel. Imagination can also have an impact on the physical state of the body, as memories and images can evoke sights, smells, sounds and feelings which can excite or calm various systems and tense or relax the heart and muscles.

A self-help technique using the imaginative channel: learning from dreams. Dreams can indicate at a symbolic level the state of our subconscious health and where we are at particular points in our life. Within them can also be found the seeds of possible solutions. It is not always possible to learn from dreams without help. This 'subject – object' technique provides a simple method for the times when we can work on them alone. If you awake from a dream feeling tense, anxious and fearful, it is worth looking to see what there is to learn from the dream about our subconscious fears and perceived inability to cope. First identify the subject of the dream (usually yourself), then the object (a person or situation). Examine the movement between the two and see if it correlates with any situation or person that you are currently dealing with. Now explore how you would like the dream to change. You can also develop or change the dream in your imagination if you wish.

> A carer dreamt that a unicorn was standing on a hill and saw a lion in the bushes below. The unicorn was very small and frightened; the lion very large and hungry. The carer woke from her dream in a state of fear. In her work on the dream, she changes the subject, the unicorn, into a large fully grown animal and the object, the lion, into a small, less frightening and less hungry lion. As the shift took place, the dreamer began to recognise strengths she had hitherto discounted. Her feelings of impotence had created a perceived enormity in the situation she was facing at work. Once she began to see the situation more realistically, strategies for dealing with it became more obvious.

Other coping strategies using this channel include guided imagery, the use of metaphors, story-telling and creative arts.

Cognition

This channel is the channel of the intellect, reflecting the work of the cognitive schools of psychology which give a high priority to mental processes such as thinking, information gathering/processing and problem solving. Under stress all these functions can become distorted. Facts mixed up with fantasy, emotion and rumour can lead to incorrect judgements and actions being made, which create opportunities for secondary problems. Techniques such as stress debriefing will help a person reorganise their cognitive functions and improve problem solving and prioritising. Information gathered about trauma, loss and grief beforehand will also aid coping afterwards.

A self-help technique using the cognitive channel: step by step problem solving.

Take a large sheet of paper.

List all the problems you think you have to solve.

Briefly define each problem. If you decide it is not really your problem or it is one you can do nothing about, cross it out.

Choose one problem at a time – either the most urgent or one you think you can solve easily.

For each problem, write down as fast as possible, all the solutions you can think of, however crazy they may seem. Crazy ideas often generate a solution that works. You can also ask other people for their ideas or find out if anyone else has had a similar problem.

Try out the solution that you feel has the best chance of working. If it doesn't, try another.

A quicker method when faced with a seemingly insoluble problem is to think through all the times when you have dealt successfully with difficult situations. This will help you to feel more positive and confident and might also generate some solutions.

Physical

Stress, trauma and loss is a physical as well as a psychological experience. Neurochemical changes can be triggered which cause physical sensations such as pains, dizziness or muscle cramps. Sudden surges of adrenalin followed by a slump can, for example, make a stressed person first hyperactive and then lethargic. These unfamiliar physical changes can in themselves cause emotional reactions and anxiety in a person. Psychologists such as Pavlov, Watson and Skinner believed that all human behaviour could be explained in physical terms through understanding neurochemical chains of reaction and the way we perceive the world through our senses and respond through our motor system. Coping methods using this channel include all forms of relaxation and breathing exercises, dance and movement (with connections here with emotional and spiritual channels), touch, physical activities, proper rest and nourishment. In situations of extreme restlessness, short bursts of energetic exercise, or even vigorous dusting and sweeping, can release tension. Most important during stress is establishing a regular achievable daily routine giving attention to sleep (stress is physically exhausting), diet, exercise (even if only a 10 minute walk), relaxation and non-stressful human contact. Excess alcohol, drugs, nicotine, under and over-eating can all exacerbate the physical changes caused by stress. A stressed person is also vulnerable to addiction.

A self-help technique using the physical channel: breathing. During times of stress the best techniques are usually the simplest. It is also easier if some techniques have been learned earlier and practised regularly, for example some relaxation methods. One of the simplest and most important techniques to remember is to do with breathing. People under stress often forget to breathe properly. It helps you first create an atmosphere which is relaxing and pampering to yourself. Candlelight and aromatic oils, especially in a bathroom or bedroom can be very effective. Then inhale through the nose, filling your body with air like a balloon so that your stomach pushes out. Then breathe out through the mouth, noticing how the muscles involved begin to relax. If you have aches and pains imagine the air and therefore oxygen being directed to that part of your body.

With practice, preparation and training, carers can develop a whole tool-bag of self-help techniques for all kinds of situations and times, and as a consequence they can enable those they care for to develop their own.

Conclusion

Our conclusion is simple. The more we are prepared for a healthy, balanced and socially orientated way of living in which we develop ourselves and our useful contributions to the good of society, the more skills we shall have to offer at times of crisis. Rather than wait for a crisis to occur before learning the skills of coping, prepare now. Death can be a great consultant for life, but fully engaging in life can be the best preparation for coping with loss.

References

Bohm, D. (1992) *Thought as a System*. London: Routledge.

Capewell, E. (1992) The clash of the gods. *Association of Counselling at Work News* **June**: 14.

Gibbs, G. (1988) *Learning by Doing. A Guide to Teaching and Learning Methods*. Oxford: Further Education Unit, Oxford Polytechnic.

Harper, J. Reaching out: running a staff care service in the aftermath of a disaster. In T. Newburn. Ed, *Working with disaster – Social Welfare Interventions During and After Tragedy*, Harlow: Longman.

Hawkins, P. and Shohet, R. (1989) *Supervision in the Helping Profession. An Individual, Group and Organisational Approach*. Milton Keynes: Open University Press.

Johnson, K. (1993) *School Crisis Management*. Alameda, California: Hunter House.

Kfir, N. (1989) *Crisis Intervention Verbatim*. New York: Hemisphere.

Lahad, M. (1993) BASIC-Ph-The story of Coping. In M. Lahad and A. Cohen (Eds) *Community Stress Prevention, Volume 2*. Kiryat Shmona, Israel: The Community Stress Prevention Centre.

Useful Organisations

The wide range of resources reflects the variety of losses and associated difficulties that can be experienced by children and the diversity of help that may be needed.

Children and Addictions

Families Anonymous
The Doddington and Rollo Community Centre, Charlotte Despart Avenue, Battersea, London, SW11 5JE.
Tel: 0171 4984680
Self-help groups throughout the United Kingdom offer help to the families and friends of people who engage in the use of mind altering substances, including alcohol.

Scottish Drugs Forum
5, Oswald Street, Glasgow, G1 4QR.
Tel: 0141 2211175
An information and policy agency which can provide details of services available in Scotland to children who are addicted themselves or affected by other people's addiction.

SCAD
Support for Children Affected by Drink
10, Samsome Place, Worcester, WR1 1UA.
Tel: 01905 23060
Helpline: 0800 318272
Offers support to children who are affected by their own or other people's drinking problems.

Alateen
61, Great Dover Street, London, SE1 4YF.
Tel: 0171 4030888
Alateen is part of the Al-Anon fellowship of family groups offering support to families and friends of people with drinking problems. Alateen is especially for teenagers who are or who have been affected by other people's drinking problems. Support is offered by local groups throughout the United Kingdom and Ireland.

Re-solv
Society for the Prevention of Solvent and Volatile Substance Abuse
30a, High Street, Stone, Staffordshire, ST15 8AW.
Tel: 01785 817885
Offers information and advice to children, parents and professionals. Operates a referral service for those requesting counselling. Produces a wide range of publications. Undertakes research and provides training for professionals. Requests for assistance should be made in writing.

UK Forum on Young People and Gambling
PO Box 5, Chichester, West Sussex, PO19 3RB.
Tel: 01243 538635
Offers information, advice and practical help to children involved in gambling or electronic game playing, their parents and professionals. Produces a newsletter and other publications. Provides courses and workshops for children and professionals.

Children and Adoption and Fostering

British Agencies for Adoption and Fostering
Skyline House, 200, Union Street, London, SE1 0LX.
Tel: 0171 5932000
Promotes public understanding of adoption and fostering and is a

major source of information for would-be adopters and foster parents. Produces a journal, books and training materials.

Post-Adoption Centre
5, Torriano Avenue, London. NW5 2RZ.
Tel: 0171 2840555
Adviceline: 0171 2840555 10.30 a.m.–1.30 p.m. Mon–Fri except
5.30 p.m.–7.30 p.m. Thur
Runs workshops and offers advice and counselling to anyone involved in adoption (birth parents, adoptive parents, adopted children and professionals).

After Adoption
Canterbury House, 12–14, Chapel Street, Salford, Manchester, M3 7NN.
Tel: 0161 8394932
Helpline: 0161 8394930
Provides post-adoption support and counselling to all parties involved in adoption, including adoptions involving families from different cultures.

National Foster Care Association
Leonard House, 5–7, Marshalsea Road, London, SE1 1EP.
Tel: 0171 8286266
Adviceline: 0171 3788015 1.00 p.m.–4.30 p.m. Mon–Fri except
Wed.
Offers information, advice and support to foster carers and professionals. Produces training packs and other resources.

Children and Advocacy

Advice Advocacy and Representation Services for Children
Canterbury House, 1–3 Greengate, Salford, Manchester, M3 7NN.
Tel: 0161 8398442
Helpline: 0800 616101
An advocacy service for children who do not feel that they are being listened to or consulted about decisions concerning their lives. Provides professionals and others with information and training.

Young People First
207–215 King's Cross Road, London, WC1X 9DB.

Tel: 0171 7136400
A self-advocacy organisation for young people with learning difficulties (16–30 year olds) with groups throughout the United Kingdom. Operates under the auspices of People First. Runs workshops and produces publications to help young people with learning difficulties and those who work with them deal with a variety of topics, including: sex and relationships, parents, jobs and money, assertiveness, being independent, taking responsibility and making choices.

Children and Appearance

Changing Faces
1–2, Junction Mews, Paddington, London, W2 1PN.
Tel: 0171 7064232
Offers information, advice and counselling to people who have a facial disfigurement and their families; a specialist service is available to children. Provides a range of activities including arranging pen pals and conducting workshops for children starting/changing school. Training programmes are available to health professionals, teachers and employers.

Disfigurement Guidance Centre
PO Box 7, Cupar, Fife, KY15 4PF.
Tel: 01334 839084
Offers information and advice to children and adults whose appearance is altered because of skin disfigurement or for other reasons. Produces a newsletter and other publications including 'A Skin Laser Directory' and 'A National Disfigurement Register'. Undertakes research and runs conferences and workshops for professionals. Correspondents should provide a stamped and self-addressed envelope.

Children and Bullying

Anti-Bullying Campaign
10, Borough Road, London, SE1 9QQ.
Tel: 0171 3781446
Offers information, advice and support to parents of bullied children and children themselves. Provides training to help teachers and others deal with bullying.

Children in Care

The Who Cares Trust
Kemp House, 152–160, City Road, London, EC1V 2NP.
Tel: 0171 2513117
0500 564570
Offers counselling and provides children and professionals with information and advice on health, education and employment. Produces a newsletter ('Who Cares') to help children in care develop in safe and healthy ways. Works to influence policy and practice affecting children in care.

The National Leaving Care Advisory Service (First Key)
Oxford Chambers, Oxford Place, Leeds, LS1 3AX.
Tel: 0113 2443898
The London Voluntary Sector Resource Centre, 356, Holloway Road, London, N7 6PA.
Tel: 0171 7000100
Provides service providers and other professionals with information and advice to help children leaving care. Works with local authorities and voluntary organisations to inform policy and practice and develop standards for service.

The Advocacy Unit of The Children's Society
14, Cathedral Road, Cardiff, CF1 9LJ.
Tel: 01222 668956
Offers advice and support to children in care or who are accommodated by social services. Help is provided only if requested by the child.

Children as Carers

Carers National Association
20–25, Glasshouse Yard, London, EC1A 4JS.
Tel: 0171 4908818
Offers information and advice to carers of different cultures and all ages. Produces a newsletter ('Link') especially for young carers and a 'Young Carer Information Pack' for those between the ages of 12 and 18 years. Young Carers Projects around the country provide advocacy, support and social activities. Provides training for professionals to help them understand the needs of carers. Undertakes research and campaigns to raise public and professional awareness and influence policy and practice.

Children and Crime

Victim Support
(England, Wales and Northern Ireland)
Cranmer House, 39, Brixton Road, London, SW9 6DZ.
Tel: 0171 7359166

Victim Support
(Scotland)
14, Frederick Street, Edinburgh, EH2 2HB.
Tel: 0131 2257779
A national network of local Victim Support schemes offers information, practical help and emotional support to victims of crime. Children under 17 will not usually be seen without the consent of a parent.

Children and Crisis

Centre for Crisis Management and Education
Elizabeth Capewell, Roselyn House, 93, Old Newtown Road,
Newbury, Berkshire, RG14 7DE.
Tel: 01635 30644
Provides consultancy, training, team development and post-trauma services to groups and organisations.

Children and Death

National Association of Bereavement Services
20, Norton Folgate, London, E1 6DB.
Tel: 0171 2470617
A national organisation with regional representation and which refers bereaved people to the nearest and most appropriate bereavement services. The Association is contacted by many children who find themselves comforting a surviving parent and looking after siblings. Provides for the needs of ethnic groups and assists during major disasters. Offers training and produces a 'National Directory of Bereavement and Loss Services' as well as other publications.

The Child Bereavement Trust
1, Millside, Riversdale, Bourne End, Buckinghamshire, SL8 5EB.
Tel: 01494 765001
Provides bereaved families with information and support. Offers specialised training, support and resources to professionals involved with grieving families.

The Compassionate Friends
53, North Street, Bristol, BS3 1EN.
Tel: 0117 9665202
Helpline: 0117 9539639
A nationwide organisation of bereaved parents offering support to other bereaved parents and siblings. Produces a newsletter and SIBBS (Support In Bereavement for Brothers and Sisters). A range of publications (including a postal library of over 700 books) is available to bereaved parents, professionals and others.

Cruse-Bereavement Care
126, Sheen Road, Richmond, Surrey, TW9 1UR.
Tel: 0181 9404818
Helpline: 0181 3327227
An organisation with branches throughout the United Kingdom offering help to bereaved people of any age; some branches provide a counselling service especially for children. Produces a newsletter and list of relevant publications. Provides training and runs workshops and seminars.

Children and Despair/Suicide

Samaritans
10, The Grove, Slough, Berkshire, SL1 1QP.
Tel: 01753 532713
Helpline: 0345 909090
Branches throughout the United Kingdom and Ireland offer a 24 hour free and confidential service to people of any age who are in despair.

Children and Difficulties of any Kind

Childline
Royal Mail Building, Studd Street, London, N1 OQW.
Tel: 0171 2391000
Helpline: 0800 1111 and Freepost 1111, London, N1 OBR.
Helpline for children in care: 0800 884444 6 p.m.–10 p.m.
Helpline for children with impaired hearing: 0800 400222 2
p.m.–9 p.m.
A national, free and confidential helpline for children in trouble or danger.

Youth Access
Ashby House, 62a, Ashby Road, Loughborough, Leicestershire, LE11 3AE.
Tel: 01509 210420
An umbrella organisation representing 200 centres throughout the United Kingdom offering information, advice and counselling to children and young adults up to 25 years old. Organises national training workshops.

NCH Action for Children
85, Highbury Park, London, N5 1UD.
Tel: 0171 2262033
Operates community-based projects and services throughout the United Kingdom for children and families in need. These include services related to: sexual abuse, children with disabilities, residential homes and schools, children leaving care, the young homeless, young offenders, and family and community centres.

Exploring Parenthood
4, Ivory Place, 20a, Treadgold Street, London, W11 4BP.
Tel: 0171 2214471
Adviceline: 0171 2216681
Offers telephone information, advice and counselling to parents who are facing problems with their children's behaviour.

Trust for the Study of Adolescence
23, New Road, Brighton, West Sussex, BN1 1WZ.
Tel: 01273 693311
Promotes the study of adolescence and a better understanding of this stage of development. Undertakes applied research, consultancy and training related to a wide range of issues, including: teenage parenthood, counselling of adolescents, adolescent mental health, and young offenders. Produces training materials for

professionals and parents, including packs on suicide and self-harm, and working with young offenders.

"Being Yourself"
Deal, Kent, CT1A 7NN.
Tel: 01304 381333
Provides educational support materials, including therapeutic games, to help children, older people and the professionals who work with them deal with difficult and distressing situations. A wide range of topics is covered, including: child protection and abuse, parenting, self-esteem, attention deficit disorders, death, serious illness, mental and physical disabilities, traumatic events, divorce, remarriage, and learning about feelings.

Adlerian Workshops and Publications
216 Tring Road, Aylesbury, Bucks, HP20 1JS
Tel: 01296 82148
Offer training, resource material and consultancy covering a range of topics for parents, young people and professionals. These include grief and bereavement, crisis intervention and understanding and coping with relationships under stress.

Children and Education

Centre for Children's Counselling and Educational Support
14, Basil Avenue, Armthorpe, Doncaster, DN3 2AT.
Tel: 01302 833596
Offers information, advice and counselling to children and parents on a range of topics, including: self-esteem, bullying, school phobias, home education, childhood anxiety, stress and depression. Runs courses for parents and professionals. Produces training packs and other resources for professionals to use with children.

Skill
National Bureau for Students with Disabilities
336, Brixton Road, London, SW9 7AA.
Tel: 0171 9789890
An information and advice service on all aspects of education, training and careers for people (16 years old and above) who have physical and/or learning disabilities.

The National Association for Gifted Children
Park Campus, Boughton Green Road, Northampton, NN2 7AL.

Tel: 01604 792300
Branches throughout the United Kingdom offer information, advice
and counselling to parents and children. Courses and activities for
children are also provided.

Children and HIV/AIDS

Positive Partners/Positively Children
Unit F7, Shakespeare Commercial Centre, 245a, Coldharb-
our Lane, London, SW9 8RR.
Tel: 0171 7387333
Positively Children operates under the auspices of Positively Partners and offers information, advice and support to children under
18 who have or who are otherwise affected by HIV/AIDS.

Children and Homelessness

The Children's Society
Edward Rudolf House, Margery Street, London, WC1X OJL.
Tel: 0171 8374299
Among its many other projects, provides refuge accommodation at
centres throughout England and Wales and operates outreach
schemes for children who have runaway from home or local authority care. Children are offered support to help them deal with the
difficulties that have caused them to runaway.

Centrepoint
Bewlay House, 2, Swallow Place, London, W1R 7AA.
Tel: 0171 6292229
Aims to ensure no children are at risk because they do not have a
safe place to stay. Provides short, medium and long term accommodation for homeless 16–25 year olds in the London area and an
emergency refuge for under 16 year olds.

Children and Illness

Action for Sick Children
Argyle House, 29–31, Euston Road, London, NW1 2SD.
Tel: 0171 8332041
A partnership of parents and health care professionals which
campaigns for better services for sick children in hospital and at

home. Provides information, advice and support to parents and professionals.

In Touch
10, Norman Road, Sale, Cheshire, M33 3DF.
Tel: 0161 9052440
Offers information to parents, voluntary organisations and professionals caring for children with rare physical and/or mental health disorders. Operates a link scheme for children and parents. Produces a newsletter and other publications including a comprehensive directory of relevant organisations.

Contact a Family
170, Tottenham Court Road, London, W1P OHA.
Tel: 0171 3833555
A national organisation which supports families whose children have disabilities and special needs. Provides information and support and links similarly situated families. Produces a newsletter and other publications. Runs workshops for parents, siblings, other family members and professionals.

Children with Learning Disabilities and Loss

Working Party on Looking at Loss and People with Learning Disabilities
National Association of Bereavement Services
20, Norton Folgate, London, E1 6DB.
Tel: 0171 2470617
Aims to raise the awareness of professional carers and others to the needs of children and adults who have learning disabilities and are experiencing loss and grief.

Department of Psychiatry of Disability
St. George's Hospital Medical School, Cranmer Terrace, London, SW17 ORE.
Tel: 0181 7255501
Produces a series of books, 'Beyond Words', which use colour, mime and symbol to explain the difficult things of life (including change, loss and grief) to people with learning disabilities. These materials can also be used as an aid to counselling. A training pack for professionals involved in helping people with learning disabilities to grieve is also available.

Children and Legal Matters

Children's Legal Centre
**University of Essex, Wivenhoe Park, Colchester, Essex, CO4
3SQ.**
Tel: 01206 872466
Adviceline: 01206 873820
Provides children and parents with free, confidential advice by
letter and telephone on all aspects of law and policy affecting
children in England and Wales. Produces a range of publications
including a monthly bulletin. Undertakes research and campaigns
to influence policy and practice.

Children and Marital Difficulties

National Family Mediation
9, Tavistock Place, London, WC1H 9SN.
Tel: 0171 3835993
Together with the many affiliated local mediation services offers
help to couples who are in the process of separation or divorce.
Mediation aims to help couples to settle some of their disputes,
particularly about arrangements for their children.

Children and Mental Health

Young Minds
102–108, Clerkenwell Road, London, EC1M 5SA.
Tel: 0171 3368445
Aims to increase public awareness of the needs of children who have
mental health problems or who are related to someone who has.
Offers information and advice to parents, professionals and others.
Produces publications including 'Does someone in your family have
a serious mental health problem' which is aimed at 12 to 16 year
olds.

Children and One-parent Families

National Council for One-Parent Families
255, Kentish Town Road, London, NW5 2LX.
Tel: 0171 2671361
Produces information booklets and other publications for single

parents. Provides a referral service to put families in contact with other agencies.

Gingerbread
16–17, Clerkenwell Close, London, EC1R OAA.
Tel: 0171   3368183
Adviceline: 0171   3368184
Self-help groups throughout the United Kingdom offer social support to single parents and their children. Operates an adviceline for legal and welfare matters.

Children and the Penal System

Prisoners' Wives and Families Society
254, Caledonian Road, Islington, London, N1 ONG.
Tel: 0171   2783981
Offers help to the families and friends of those who are or who have been in prison or received non-custodial sentences. Assists with the maintenance of family relationships during periods of separation. Provides information and advice. Operates a referral service for those requesting counselling. Provides financial support in the form of one-off crisis payments for children.

National Association for Care and Resettlement of Offenders
Youth Crime Section
169, Clapham Road, London, SW9 OPU.
Tel: 0171   5826500
Works to influence policy and practice regarding young offenders. Provides information and advice to professionals.

Children and Personal Safety

Kidscape
152, Buckingham Palace Road, London, SW1W 9TR.
Tel: 0171   7303300
Provides parents and children with written materials and videos to promote personal safety during childhood. Topics dealt with include: bullying, keeping safe and sexual abuse. Produces a range of teaching resources for professionals to use with children.

Children and Poverty

Child Poverty Action Group
1–5, Bath Street, London, EC1V 9PY.
Tel: 0171 2533406
A national campaigning body concerned with poverty and families. Offers information and advice to welfare rights advisors. Produces publications on welfare rights and research into poverty. Runs courses on welfare rights.

Children and Self-esteem

Self-Esteem Network
31, Carisbrooke Road, London, E17 7EF.
Tel: 0181 5216977
Affiliated to the International Council for Self-Esteem and set up to promote self-esteem in policy and practice. The following activities are either underway or planned: newsletter, workshops, directory of materials, list of trainers and courses, self-esteem audit for organisations, local self-esteem circles.

Murray White
5, Ferry Path, Cambridge, CB4 1HB.
Tel: 01223 365351
A member of the International Council for Self-Esteem and a leading author on self-esteem. Presents workshops and produces materials aimed at increasing self-esteem in children. Originator of Circletime – a programme to enhance self-esteem by enabling school children to be in touch with and give expression to their feelings.

Children and Sexual Abuse

Standing Committee on Sexually Abused Children
73, St. Charles Square, London, W10 6EJ.
Tel and Adviceline: 0181 9606376
Offers support services to professionals and all workers in the field of sexual abuse by providing training, consultancy, information and resources. Operates an adviceline ('Sounding Board') for professionals.

Children and Stepfamilies

National Stepfamily Association
Chapel House, 18, Hatton Place, London, EC1N 8RU.
Tel: 0171 2092460
Helpline: 0171 2092464
Offers information, advice and support to all members of stepfamilies and those who work with them. Produces a newsletter and other publications. Encourages research on remarriage and represents the concerns of stepfamilies to policymakers.

Index